我们说中文
We Speak Chinese

课本　中级 1
Textbook　Intermediate 1

宋可音 (Ko-Yin Sung)　编著

北京大学出版社
PEKING UNIVERSITY PRESS

图书在版编目(CIP)数据

我们说中文.中级1/宋可音编著.—北京：北京大学出版社，2013.9
ISBN 978-7-301-22961-3

Ⅰ.我…　Ⅱ.宋…　Ⅲ.汉语–对外汉语教学–教材　Ⅳ.H195.4

中国版本图书馆CIP数据核字(2013)第183246号

书　　　　名：	我们说中文·中级1
著作责任者：	宋可音　编著
责 任 编 辑：	沈　岚
标 准 书 号：	ISBN 978-7-301-22961-3/H·3354
出 版 发 行：	北京大学出版社
地　　　　址：	北京市海淀区成府路205号　100871
电　　　　话：	邮购部 62752015　发行部 62750672　编辑部 62767349　出版部 62754962
网　　　　址：	http://www.pup.cn　新浪微博:@北京大学出版社
电 子 信 箱：	zpup@pup.pku.edu.cn
印　 刷　 者：	北京大学印刷厂
经　销　者：	新华书店
	889毫米×1194毫米　大16开本　14.25印张　430千字
	2013年9月第1版　2013年9月第1次印刷
定　　　　价：	85.00元(课本、练习册全2册，含1张MP3光盘)

未经许可，不得以任何方式复制或抄袭本书之部分或全部内容。
版权所有，侵权必究
举报电话：010-62752024　电子信箱：fd@pup.pku.edu.cn

目 录
Contents

前言 ·· 1
Preface ·· 4

词性缩略语 ·· 1
Abbreviations of Parts of Speech

第一课　你暑假过得怎么样? ································ 1
Lesson 1　How Did Your Summer Vacation Go?

第二课　我们保持联络! ·· 16
Lesson 2　Let's Keep in Touch!

第三课　你们准备好点菜了吗? ······························ 31
Lesson 3　Are You Ready to Order?

第四课　我迷路了 ·· 46
Lesson 4　I am Lost on the Road

第五课　春夏秋冬 ·· 59
Lesson 5　Spring, Summer, Autumn and Winter

第六课　你妈妈要你买什么? ·································· 72
Lesson 6　What Did Your Mom Ask You to Buy?

第七课　动物园 ·· 86
Lesson 7　The Zoo

第八课　我生病了 ·· 101
Lesson 8　I am Sick

第九课　　拆礼物 ··· 114
Lesson 9　　Unwrapping Gifts

第十课　　新年快乐 ··· 128
Lesson 10　　Happy New Year

繁体情景对话课文 ··· 142
Lesson Scenarios in Traditional Chinese Characters

词汇表 ··· 154
Vocabulary Glossary

前 言

介绍

该系列教材分为两级,共有四册课本和练习册。

课本	练习册
初级一	初级一
初级二	初级二
中级一	中级一
中级二	中级二

课本和练习册配合使用。该系列教材主要是为汉语为第二语言的初中生和高中生设计的。当然,这套教材也可以作为大学一年级汉语课程的补充教材或也可以用于大学的汉语会话及文化课程。

初级一和初级二适用于第一年学习汉语的中学生。中级一和中级二则适用于第二年学习汉语的中学生。教师可自己做判断,并考虑到课程时间长短和学习者的能力。

该系列教材的设计理念是以培养语言交际能力作为重点。教学以沟通的有效性为主要目的,而不是语法结构的讲解。旨在帮助学习者以口语和书面语的形式用目标语中文与他人沟通。主题的选择是调查了约100名美国中学生最喜欢的中文教材后决定的。

课本的结构

初级一第一课主要为介绍汉语拼音,第二课主要为介绍汉字系统。其余课基本包括以下几个部分:

沟通任务:列出学习者在学完本课后能应用在日常生活中的功能点。

课前讨论:课前讨论列出的问题能让老师知道学习者对每课主题的了

解程度。这些问题可以帮助老师决定花多少时间为学习者建立主题的背景知识。虽然列出的问题是英文,如果学习者对每课的主题准备充分,老师也可鼓励学习者试着用目标语中文来沟通。

生词:这一部分列出了课文里使用的词汇(包括专有名词)。简体和繁体汉字一并列出。另外,词语的拼音、词性以及例句也包括在表中。

补充词语:这个部分列出了口语沟通活动和读写沟通活动里所使用的词汇。为了让学生增加词汇量,此部分的词汇量没有有意控制。补充词语学多学少由老师按照学生的程度决定。

沟通任务:这一部分列出了课文情景的主要语言点。这一部分不用传统语法的教学方式来讲解。此部分介绍了每个沟通任务及例句,并请学习者与同学一起进行沟通练习。

情景:情景包含了每课的课文内容。每个情景展示了之前所介绍的词汇和沟通任务。并引导学生学习如何在不同的情景下进行有效的会话,此部分显示的不同情景有助于培养学习者对目标语中文的语感。

口语沟通活动:此部分提供了学习者尝试运用刚学到的语言知识练习口头表达能力的机会。以交际语言教学法为原则,设计了不同情景让学习者用目标语中文做有意义的会话练习。与强调演练或记忆词汇的活动相比,此书的沟通活动可以更有效地帮助学习者提高语言交际能力。

读写沟通活动:此部分与口语沟通活动采用相同的设计理念,只是着重于学习者阅读和写作技能的训练。

讨论:此部分介绍有关的中国文化。讨论的主题与每课的主题相关。列出的讨论问题使老师与学生进一步理解中国文化。

练习册的结构

初级一第一课为汉语拼音练习,第二课为汉字知识的练习。其余课基本包括以下几个部分:听力练习、口语练习、阅读练习、写作练习和沟通练习。前四个练习中的每一个练习分别侧重于听、说、读、写这四种语言技能中的一种,最后一个练习是这四种语言技能的综合练习。

给教师的话

使用本系列教材的教师应注重第二语言通过沟通任务的习得。换句话说,学生在类似于现实生活情景的课堂活动中(例如:小组讨论、模拟和角色扮演)学习汉语。这也是本系列教材所倡导的教学法。当学习者做练习时,教师应支持和帮助学生构建目标语中文的语言知识,从而使他们逐渐成为独立的学习者。

致谢

　　首先感谢北京大学出版社出版《我们说中文》这一系列教材,使我有机会实践我对汉语教学的想法。同时感谢王飙主任的专业指导和支持。另外,我也要感谢丈夫罗蓝登、母亲曾淑玲和父亲宋总男对我的鼓励和支持!

Introduction

This book series consists of four textbooks and workbooks in two levels:

Textbook	Workbook
Beginner 1	Beginner 1
Beginner 2	Beginner 2
Intermediate 1	Intermediate 1
Intermediate 2	Intermediate 2

Each textbook is combined with its workbook into a single book. This series is designed mainly for middle and high school students who study Chinese as a second or foreign language. The beginner books can be used as supplementary materials for first-year Chinese at the collegiate level. Also, the intermediate books can be used in a college Chinese conversation or culture course.

In a middle or high school, the beginner books are suitable for use in first-year Chinese while the intermediate books are suitable for use in second-year Chinese. However, teachers need to make their own judgment, taking into consideration the class time period, how the books are used, and the ability of learners. The design of this book series uses the communicative language learning and teaching approaches as the guide. The series focuses on the effectiveness of communication rather than the practice of grammatical patterns. The goal is to assist learners in successfully communicating with others in the target language, Mandarin Chinese, in both oral and written forms. The topic of each lesson was carefully selected based on survey results

Preface

of approximately 100 American middle and high school students' most desirable Chinese textbook topics.

Structure of the Textbook

Except Lesson 1, which introduces the phonetic system, pinyin, and Lesson 2, which discusses the Chinese writing system, each lesson consists of the following sections:

Communicative Tasks: This section identifies structures learners will study in the lesson and be able to apply in daily life after learning the lesson.

Warm-up Discussion Questions: The warm-up questions are used to learn how much background knowledge learners may have in regard to the lesson topic. It is used as a way to connect with learners' own experiences and help instructors decide how much time should be spent building on learners' background knowledge for the lesson. Although the questions are in English, teachers can encourage students to try to use the target language to communicate if they have enough background knowledge and are familiar with the topic.

Vocabulary: The vocabulary chart in the Vocabulary section illustrates the vocabulary words used in the lesson texts in the Scenarios section. The vocabulary words are shown in both simplified and traditional Chinese characters. In addition, the pinyin of the words and examples of how to use the words are included in the chart.

Supplementary Vocabulary: The vocabulary chart in the Supplementary Vocabulary section includes vocabulary words used in the Oral and Literacy Communication Activities sections. The number of vocabulary in each lesson is not purposely controlled. Teachers can decide how to learn the supplementary vocabulary depending on the learners' language level.

Communicative Tasks: This section lists the main structures used in the Scenarios section. The traditional grammar methods are not used to introduce the structures. Instead, the communicative goal of each structure is identified, examples of how to use the structures are given, and learners are asked to try out the structures with classmates.

Scenarios: The Scenarios section contains the main texts of the lesson. Each scenario in the section provides examples of how the structures and vocabulary words introduced in the previous sections can be used in a particular context. A competent speaker is expected to know what to say to others appropriately in any situation. Hence, showing how the structures are used in different scenarios helps develop learners' target language knowledge and communicative competence.

Oral Communication Activities: This section provides learners opportunities to try out the newly learned language knowledge with a focus on oral skills. Drawing upon the principle of Communicative Language Learning, the oral activities in this section are designed as communicative tasks in which certain scenarios are created in order for students to work collaboratively to interact in the target language with the focus on meaning rather than form. Compared to activities which emphasize drills or memorizing vocabulary and structures, the communicative activities in this textbook can more effectively help learners use the target language appropriately in real life situations.

Literacy Communication Activities: This section adopts the same activity design principle mentioned in the previous section except that this section focuses on the practice of reading and writing.

Discussion: This section introduces aspects of Chinese culture. The topic varies in each lesson, but is closely related to the lesson topic. The discussion questions listed in this section provide instructors a starting point for a cultural discussion with their learners to help them gain cultural knowledge of the target language.

Structure of the Workbook

Except Lesson 1, which contains exercises of the pinyin system, and Lesson 2, which has exercises of the knowledge of Chinese characters, each lesson consists of the following sections: Listening Exercise, Speaking Exercise, Reading Exercise, Writing Exercise, and Communicative Exercise. Each of the first four exercises focuses on one of the four language skills while the last exercise provides practice of a combination of language skills.

Notes to Teachers

Teachers who use this book series should keep in mind that second language acquisition develops through communicative tasks. In other words, students learn through class activities which are similar to real-life situations, such as group discussions, real-life simulations, and role-play, all of which this book series advocates and provides. When learners carry out the activities, teachers should work as facilitators to support language development while their students move progressively to independent learners.

Acknowledgments

I would like to express my gratitude to Peking University Press for offering me the opportunity of implementing my Chinese language teaching and learning ideas in this textbook series. Many thanks go to the director, Biao Wang, for his professional guidance and continuous support. I would also like to thank my significant other, Brendan, and my parents, Shuling and Tsungnan, who have always encouraged me to pursue my work on this series.

词性缩略语
Abbreviations of Parts of Speech

Abbreviation	Definition
n.	noun
v.	verb
pron.	pronoun
adj.	adjective
adv.	adverb
part.	particle
conj.	conjunction
m.w.	measure word
num.	number
suff.	suffix
prep.	preposition
aux.	auxiliary
int.	interrogative
v.o.	verb object
interj.	interjection
pre.	prefix
p.n.	proper nouns

第一课 Lesson 1

你暑假过得怎么样?
How Did Your Summer Vacation Go?

沟通任务 Communication Tasks

- Asking how one's summer vacation went.
- Asking how one did at work.
- Using the form verb + 了, to stress what one has done.
- Asking if one can teach you a certain skill.
- Asking if one has finished writing something.
- Asking how to write a specific Chinese character.
- Asking for the meaning of a Chinese word.
- Asking how to say a specific word, phrase or sentence in Chinese.
- Describing what one did before or after class.

课前讨论 Warm-up Discussion Questions

1. Did you have a great summer vacation? What did you do in the summer? Did you go to a summer camp? Did you visit your relatives?

2. Do you have questions about the Chinese language? Do you know how to ask a language question in Chinese?

3. What do you usually do before and after class?

生词 Vocabulary

简体 (Simplified)	繁体 (Traditional)	拼音 (Pinyin)	释义 (Definition)	词性 (Parts of speech)	例句 (Examples)
1. 过	過	guò	to spend	v.	我暑假过得很好。(My summer vacation went well.)
2. 城市	城市	chéngshì	city	n.	我去了很多个城市。(I went to many cities.)
3. 玩	玩	wán	to travel	v.	我们去了很多城市玩。(We traveled to many cities.)
3. 从……到……	從……到……	cóng...dào...	from...to...		我从早上十点到晚上七点都在中国餐馆工作。(I worked from 10 am to 7 pm in the Chinese restaurant.)
4. 主管	主管	zhǔguǎn	supervisor	n.	我的主管说我做得很好。(My supervisor said I did well.)
5. 不错	不錯	búcuò	not bad; pretty good	adj.	我暑假过得不错。(My summer vacation wasn't bad.)
6. 长笛	長笛	chángdí	flute	n.	我会吹长笛。(I can play the flute.)
7. 蝶泳	蝶泳	diéyǒng	butterfly stroke	n.	我学了怎么游蝶泳。(I learned how to swim the butterfly stroke.)
8. 仰泳	仰泳	yǎngyǒng	back stroke	n.	我会仰泳。(I can swim the back stroke.)
9. 交际舞	交際舞	jiāojìwǔ	ballroom dance	n.	我学了怎么跳交际舞。(I learned how to ballroom dance.)
10. 芭蕾舞	芭蕾舞	bālěiwǔ	ballet	n.	我会跳芭蕾舞。(I can dance the ballet.)
11. 才艺	才藝	cáiyì	talent; skill	n.	我学了很多才艺。(I learned many skills.)
12. 当然	當然	dāngrán	of course	adv.	你当然可以来我家。(Of course you can come to my home.)

第一课 你暑假过得怎么样?
Lesson 1 How Did Your Summer Vacation Go?

13. 一些	一些	yīxiē	some	*num.*	我有一些汉字不会写。(There are some Chinese characters I don't know how to write.)
14. 请教	請教	qǐngjiào	to ask	*v.*	我可以请教你一些问题吗? (May I ask you some questions?)
15. 还	還	hái	still	*adv.*	我还有一个问题。(I still have a question.)
16. 意思	意思	yìsi	meaning	*n.*	"你好"是什么意思? (What does "ni hao" mean?)
17. 最后	最後	zuìhòu	final; last	*n.*	这是我的最后一个问题。(This is my last question.)
18. 日记	日記	rìjì	diary	*n.*	我喜欢写日记。(I like to write in my diary.)
19. 开学日	開學日	kāixuérì	school start date	*n.*	今天是学校开学日。(Today is the school start date.)
20. 前	前	qián	before	*n.*	上课前我写了很多汉字。(Before going to class, I wrote a lot of Chinese characters.)
21. 聊天	聊天	liáo tiān	to chat		上课前我跟我的朋友们聊天。(Before going to class, I chatted with my friends.)
22. 每	每	měi	every	*pron.*	每个人暑假都过得很好。(Everybody's summer vacation went well.)
23. 下课	下課	xià kè	class dismissed		
后	後	hòu	after	*n.*	下课后我教我朋友怎么跳交际舞。(After class I taught my friends how to ballroom dance.)
24. 开心	開心	kāixīn	happy	*adj.*	我们都很开心。(We are all very happy.)
25. 再次	再次	zàicì	again	*adv*	我很高兴再次到中国旅游! (I am happy to travel in China again!)
26. 见到	見到	jiàndào	to see (people)	*v.*	今天我很高兴再次见到我的朋友们! (I am very happy to see my friends again!)

3

 专有名词 Proper Nouns

简体 (Simplified)	繁体 (Traditional)	拼音 (Pinyin)	释义 (Definition)	词性 (Parts of speech)	例句 (Examples)
1. 旧金山	舊金山	Jiùjīnshān	San Francisco	p.n.	我们去了旧金山。(We went to San Francisco.)
2. 圣地亚哥	聖地亞哥	Shèngdìyàgē	San Diego	p.n.	我们也去了圣地亚哥。(We also went to San Diego.)
3. 洛杉矶	洛杉磯	Luòshānjī	Los Angeles	p.n.	洛杉矶在加州。(Los Angeles is in California.)

 补充词语 Supplementary Vocabulary

Simplified	Traditional	Pinyin	Definition
1. 还好	還好	hái hǎo	not bad
2. 马马虎虎	馬馬虎虎	mǎmǎhūhū	so so (adj.)
3. 不太好	不太好	bú tài hǎo	not good
4. 很不好	很不好	hěn bù hǎo	very bad

 沟通任务 Communication Tasks

I Asking how one's summer vacation went

Question: 你暑假过得怎么样？(How did your summer vacation go?)
Answer: 我暑假过得_____。(My summer vacation went _____.)
Elaborated Answer: 我暑假过得_____。我_____。
        (My summer vacation went _____. I _____.)
Note:
Listed below are words you can use to describe how something went

very well	well	OK	so-so	not too well	poorly
很好	不错	还好	马马虎虎	不太好	很不好

第一课 你暑假过得怎么样？
Lesson 1 How Did Your Summer Vacation Go?

Example:

Question: 你暑假过得怎么样？
(How did your summer vacation go?)
Answer 1: 我暑假过得<u>很好</u>。 (My summer vacation went <u>very well</u>.)
Answer 2: 我暑假<u>很忙</u>。 (I had a <u>busy</u> summer vacation.)
Answer 3: 我暑假过得<u>不错</u>。 (My summer vacation <u>went well</u>.)
Elaborated Answer: 我暑假过得<u>很好</u>。我<u>去了加州看我阿姨、姨丈和表弟</u>。
(My summer vacation went <u>very well</u>. I <u>went to California to see my aunt, uncle, and cousin</u>.)

Practice: Ask your classmates how their summer vacation went.

II) Asking how one did at work

Question: 你工作做得怎么样？ (How did you do at work?)
Answer 1: 我工作做得_____。 (I did _____ at work.)
Elaborated Answer: 我的主管说我_____。
(My manager said that I _____.)

Example:

Question: 你工作做得怎么样？ (How did you do at work?)
Answer 1: 我工作做得<u>还好</u>。 (I did <u>OK</u> at work.)
Elaborated Answer: 我的主管说我<u>做得很好</u>。
(My manager said that I <u>did very well</u>.)

Practice: Do any of your classmates work part-time? Ask them how they did at work.

III) Using "verb+了" to stress what one has done

Using the verb 学 as an example
我学了_____。 (I learned _____.)

Examples:

我学了<u>很多才艺</u>。 (I learned <u>a lot of skills</u>.)
我学了<u>怎么吹长笛</u>。 (I learned <u>how to play the flute</u>.)

Practice: What skills have you learned recently? Tell your class.

IV) Asking if one can teach you a certain skill

Question: 你可以教我们怎么_____吗？
(Can you teach us how to _____?)

Positive Answer: 当然可以。(Of course I can.)

Negative Answer: 对不起,我_____。(Sorry, but I _____.)

Example:

Question: 你可以教我们怎么<u>跳交际舞</u>吗?

(Can you teach us how to <u>ballroom dance</u>?)

Positive Answer: 当然可以。(Of course I can.)

Negative Answer: 对不起,我<u>现在没有时间</u>。(Sorry, but I <u>don't have time now</u>.)

Practice: Ask your teacher if he or she can teach you how to speak Chinese.

V) Asking if one has finished writing something

Question: 你写完_____了吗?

(Have you finished writing _____?)

Positive Answer: 我写完了。(I have finished writing it.)

Negative Answer: 我还没有呢。(I haven't.)

Example:

Question: 你写完<u>中文暑假作业</u>了吗?

(Have you finished writing <u>your summer Chinese homework</u>?)

Positive Answer: 我写完了。(I have finished writing it.)

Negative Answer: 我还没有呢。(I haven't.)

Practice: Ask your classmates if they have finished their Chinese homework.

VI) Asking how to write a specific Chinese character

Question: "_____"的"_____"怎么写? (How do you write "_____" in "_____"?)

Answer: 我写给你看。(Let me show you.)

Example:

Question: "<u>游泳</u>"的"<u>游</u>"怎么写? (How do you write "<u>游</u>" in "<u>游泳</u>"?)

Answer: 我写给你看。(Let me show you.)

Practice: Ask a classmate sitting next to you how to write a certain Chinese character.

VII) Asking for the meaning of a Chinese word

Question: "_____"是什么意思? (What is the meaning of "_____"?)

Answer: "_____"是"_____"的意思。("_____" means "_____".)

第一课　你暑假过得怎么样？
Lesson 1　How Did Your Summer Vacation Go?

Example:

Question: "城市"是什么意思？(What is the meaning of "城市"?)
Answer: "城市"是"city"的意思。("城市" means "city".)
Practice: Pick a word you just learned in this lesson and ask a classmate the meaning of it.

VIII) Asking how to say a specific word phrase or sentence in Chinese

Question: "＿＿＿＿＿＿"中文怎么说？
　　　　　(How do you say "＿＿＿＿＿＿" in Chinese?)
Answer: ＿＿＿＿＿＿。(＿＿＿＿＿＿.)

Example:

Question: "Thanks for your help"中文怎么说？
　　　　　(How do you say "Thanks for your help" in Chinese?)
Answer: 谢谢你的帮忙。(Thanks for your help.)
Practice: Think of a word in English and ask your teacher how to say it in Chinese using "＿＿＿＿中文怎么说？"

IX) Describing what one did before or after class

上课前＿＿＿＿＿＿＿＿＿＿。(＿＿＿＿＿＿＿＿＿ before class.)
下课后＿＿＿＿＿＿＿＿＿＿。(＿＿＿＿＿＿＿＿＿ after class.)

Example:

上课前我跟朋友们聊天。(I chatted with my friends before class.)
下课后吴家玲教我们怎么跳交际舞。
(吴家玲 taught us how to ballroom dance after class.)
Practice: Tell your class what you did before class.

情景(一) Scenario 1

李小明、张爱华和吴家玲正要去饭馆庆祝李小明的生日。

吴家玲：好久不见！你们暑假过得怎么样？
张爱华：我暑假过得很好。我去了加州看我阿姨、姨丈和表弟。我们一起开车去了很多个城市玩。我们去了旧金山、圣地亚哥和洛杉矶。
李小明：我暑假很忙。我每天从早上十点到晚上七点都在中国餐馆当收银员。
吴家玲：你工作做得怎么样？

李小明：我的主管说我做得很好。我很高兴。家玲，你暑假过得怎么样？
吴家玲：我暑假过得不错。我参加了三个夏令营。我在音乐夏令营学了怎么吹长笛，在游泳夏令营学了怎么游蝶泳和仰泳，在舞蹈夏令营学了怎么跳交际舞和芭蕾舞。我学了很多才艺。
张爱华：你可以教我们怎么跳交际舞吗？
吴家玲：当然可以。

Comprehension Questions

1. 张爱华去了加州哪里玩？
2. 李小明几点到几点在中国餐馆当收银员？
3. 吴家玲暑假学了什么？

情景(二) Scenario 2

王文丽：家玲，你写完中文暑假作业了吗？
吴家玲：我写完了。你呢？
王文丽：我还没有呢。我有一些汉字不会写。我可以请教你吗？
吴家玲：当然可以。
王文丽："游泳"的"游"怎么写？
吴家玲：我写给你看。

吴家玲正在教王文丽怎么写"游"这个汉字。

王文丽：我还有一个问题。"城市"是什么意思？
吴家玲："城市"是"city"的意思。
王文丽：最后一个问题，"Thanks for your help"中文怎么说？
吴家玲："谢谢你的帮助。"
王文丽：家玲，谢谢你的帮助！
吴家玲：不客气！

Comprehension Questions

1. 吴家玲写完中文暑假作业了吗？
2. "Thanks for your help"中文怎么说？

第一课 你暑假过得怎么样?
Lesson 1 How Did Your Summer Vacation Go?

情景(三)Scenario 3

李小明正在写他的日记……

李小明的日记

今天是学校开学日。上课前我跟朋友们聊天,聊了暑假做了什么。张爱华去了加州,吴家玲参加了三个夏令营,我在中国餐馆做了收银员。每个人暑假都过得很好,也很忙。下课后吴家玲教我们怎么跳交际舞。我们都很开心。今天我很高兴再次见到我的朋友们!

Comprehension Questions

1. 李小明今天做了什么?
2. 李小明今天高兴吗?

口语沟通活动 Oral Communication Activities

I. 情况:今天是暑假后第一天上课。你想知道你的同学们暑假过得怎么样。

Situation: Today is the first day of school after summer vacation. You want to know how your classmates' summer vacation went.

任务:在教室问你的同学们,"你暑假过得怎么样?"。在下方表格写下他们的名字并勾选他们的答案。

Task: Walk around the classroom to survey your classmates by asking, "你暑假过得怎么样?". Write down their names in the table below and put a check mark under the answer they provide.

姓名	很好	不错	还好	马马虎虎	不太好	很不好
1.						
2.						
3.						
4.						
5.						
6.						

7.						
8.						
9.						
10.						

你问的几个同学中，有哪些人回答很好、不错、还好、马马虎虎、不太好或很不好？把人数写在下方表格并用以下结构在课堂上报告，"___个人暑假过得很好"，"___个人暑假过得不错"，"___个人暑假过得还好"，"___个人暑假过得马马虎虎"，"___个人暑假过得不太好"，"___个人暑假过得很不好"。

Of the people you surveyed, how many answered 很好, 不错, 还好, 马马虎虎, 不太好, or 很不好? Write down the numbers in the table below and report them to the class using the sentence structure, "___个人暑假过得很好", "___个人暑假过得不错", "___个人暑假过得还好", "___个人暑假过得马马虎虎", "___个人暑假过得不太好", "___个人暑假过得很不好".

	很好	不错	还好	马马虎虎	不太好	很不好
人数 # of people						

II. 情况：陈林和张爱友正在图书馆做他们的作业。他们各有一些问题想问对方。下方表格列出了他们的问题。

Situation: Chen Lin and Zhang Aiyou are doing their Chinese homework together in the library and each of them has questions for the other. The tables below show their questions.

陈林的问题　　Chen Lin's questions

	怎么写	是什么意思	中文怎么说
1.	"舞蹈"的"蹈"	跳舞	I learned how to dance.
2.	"攀岩"的"攀"	登山	I like rock-climbing.
3.	"暑假"的"假"	开学	My summer vacation went very well.

第一课 你暑假过得怎么样？
Lesson 1 How Did Your Summer Vacation Go?

张爱友的问题　Zhang Aiyou's questions

	怎么写	是什么意思	中文怎么说
1.	"工作"的"工"	打工	How did you do at work?
2.	"汉堡"的"堡"	猪肉汉堡	I want to eat beef burger.
3.	"夏令营"的"营"	足球夏令营	I joined three summer camps.

任务：两人一组。一个人扮演陈林，另一个人扮演张爱友。用下方的会话结构问彼此中文作业的问题。

Task: Work in pairs. One acts as Chen Lin and the other acts as Zhang Aiyou. Use the following conversation structure to ask each other questions about the Chinese homework.

会话结构：
Conversation Structure:
陈林："舞蹈"的"蹈"怎么写？
张爱友：我写给你看。

（张爱友教陈林怎么写"蹈"这个汉字）
陈林：我还有一个问题。"跳舞"是什么意思？
张爱友："跳舞"是"dance"的意思。
陈林：最后一个问题，"I learned how to dance." 中文怎么说？
张爱友："我学了怎么跳舞。"

（陈林问完了全部的问题后）
陈林：谢谢你的帮助！
张爱友：不客气！

读写沟通活动 Literacy Communication Activities

I. 陈文丽的家人在暑假学了不同的才艺。陈文丽想请他们教她这些才艺。帮助陈文丽和她的家人完成下列问题和答案。

Chen Wenli's family members learned different skills in the summer. Chen Wenli wants to ask them if they can teach her the skills. Help Chen Wenli and her family complete the questions and answers below.

陈文丽: 您可以教我怎么_____吗?
爷爷: 对不起,我_____。
　　　(I don't have time now.)

陈文丽: 您可以教我怎么_____吗?
妈妈: _____。
　　　(Of course I can.)

第一课 你暑假过得怎么样?
Lesson 1 How Did Your Summer Vacation Go?

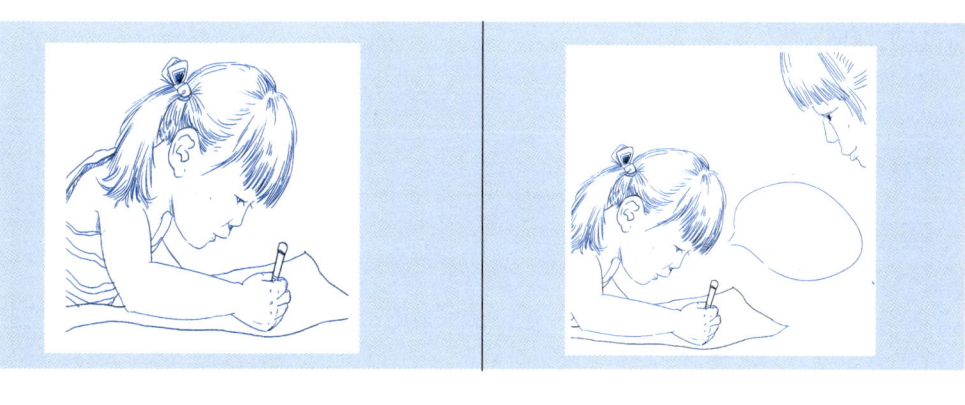

陈文丽: 你可以教我怎么_____吗?

妹妹: 对不起,我_____。
（I am busy now.）

陈文丽: 你可以教我怎么_____吗?

姐姐: _____。
（Of course I can.）

II. 你中文班的朋友们想知道你昨天上课前和下课后做了什么。在下方空格画出你上课前和下课后做的两件事并写出完整的中文句子来描述这些图。

Your friends in Chinese class want to know what you did before and after class yesterday. Draw two things you did before and after class in the spaces provided below and write complete sentences in Chinese to describe the pictures.

上课前

1.	2.

1. 上课前 _____
2. 上课前 _____

下课后

1.	2.

1. 下课后 _____
2. 下课后 _____

讨论 Discussion

Learning Chinese

Many Americans are heading to China to study the Chinese language and culture. According to the *Open Doors Report* published by the Institute of International Education, China is the fifth most popular study abroad destination for U.S. students. In 2006, more than 11,000 students went to China, an increase of 25% since 2005 (Open Doors, 2008). Moreover, the report showed that the majority of these students engaged in Chinese language study (Open Doors, 2008). There are currently hundreds of programs in China for U.S. graduate and undergraduate students offered by the U.S. and Chinese governments. In addition, there are private institutes which offer varieties of Chinese language and culture programs for students at different age levels year around.

Lesson 1 How Did Your Summer Vacation Go?
第一课 你暑假过得怎么样？

Discussion Question:

1. Have you thought about studying in China? To which city do you want to go? What places do you want to visit and what kinds of food do you want to try while you are in China?

Reference:

Open Doors (2008). *Report on International Educational Exchange.* Sewickley, PA: Institute for International Education.

第二课
Lesson 2

我们保持联络!
Let's Keep in Touch!

沟通任务 Communication Tasks

- Indicating the method of transportation to go or return to a certain place.
- Asking the question "why".
- Asking if one can do something before leaving.
- Stating what you want to do after returning to a place.
- Suggesting to write certain information on a piece of paper.
- Asking if one can see you on the computer.
- Asking if one uses a certain thing.
- Stating that you know a person in someone's friend list on Facebook.
- Stating your hope.

课前讨论 Warm-up Discussion Questions

1. Do you frequently chat with your friends online? Do you use a webcam when you chat?

2. Do you like using e-mail, instant messenger, Facebook, and a cell phone to keep in touch with your friends?

第二课 我们保持联络!
Lesson 2 Let's Keep in Touch!

生词 Vocabulary

简体 (Simplified)	繁体 (Traditional)	拼音 (Pinyin)	释义 (Definition)	词性 (Parts of speech)	例句 (Examples)
1. 溜	溜	liū	to skate	v.	我们一起溜滑板吧。(Let's go skate boarding.)
2. 飞机	飛機	fēijī	airplane	n.	我明天早上八点得坐飞机。(I have to take the airplane tomorrow at 8 am.)
3. 回	回	huí	to return	v.	我想回美国。(I want to return to the U.S.A..)
5. 为什么	為什麽	wèi shénme	why		为什么你明天要回美国？(Why do you want to return to the U.S.A. tomorrow?)
6. 下星期	下星期	xià xīngqī	next week		我的学校下星期才开学。(My school won't start until next week.)
7. 真	真	zhēn	really	adv.	你汉语说得真棒！(Your Chinese is Excellent!)
棒	棒	bàng	excellent	adj.	
8. 离开	離開	líkāi	to leave	v.	他现在不在这里，昨天下午就离开了。(He was not here now, and left yesterday afternoon.)
9. 以前	以前	yǐqián	before; in the past	n.	我离开中国以前跟我中国朋友说再见。(Before I left China, I said goodbye to my Chinese friends.)
10. 电子邮件	電子郵件	diànzǐyóujiàn	e-mail		我想给你写电子邮件。(I want to write e-mails to you.)
11. 地址	地址	dìzhǐ	address	n.	你可以给我你的地址吗？(Could you give me your address?)
12. 即时通讯	即時通訊	jíshí tōngxùn	instant messenger		你可以给我你的即时通讯账号吗？(Could you give me your instant messenger account?)

17

13. 联络	聯絡	liánluò	to contact	v.	我们也可以用即时通讯联络。(We can also use instant messenger to contact each other.)
14. 手机	手機	shǒujī	cell phone	n.	我的手机在哪儿？(Where is my cell phone?)
15. 号码	號碼	hàomǎ	number	n.	你可以给我你的手机号码吗？(Can you give me your cell phone number?)
16. 以后	以後	yǐhòu	in the future	n.	我回美国以后会打电话给你。(I will call you after I return to the U.S.A..)
17. 寄	寄	jì	to send	v.	今天我寄了一本中文书给我弟弟。(Today I sent a Chinese book to my younger brother.)
18. 张	張	zhāng	classifier for thin pieces	m.w.	我有一张红色的纸。(I have a red piece of paper.)
19. 风景	風景	fēngjǐng	scenery	n.	中国的风景明信片很好看。(Chinese scenery postcards look nice.)
20. 明信片	明信片	míngxìnpiàn	postcard	n.	这张明信片很好看。(This postcard looks nice.)
21. 纸	紙	zhǐ	paper	n.	这张纸是白的。(This piece of paper is white.)
22. 上	上	shàng	on	n.	我们把地址写在一张纸上吧。(Let's write our addresses on a piece of paper.)
23. 看得到	看得到	kàn de dào	to be able to see		你在电脑上看得到我吗？(Are you able to see me on the computer?)
24. 看不到	看不到	kàn bú dào	to be unable to see		我看不到你。(I am not able to see you.)
25. 安装	安裝	ānzhuāng	to set up	v.	我还没安装网络摄像机。(I haven't set up the webcam.)
26. 网络摄像机	網絡攝像機	wǎngluò shèxiàngjī	webcam		我安装了网络摄像机。(I have set up the webcam.)
27. 用	用	yòng	to use	v.	你用不用中文书？(Do you use Chinese books?)
28. 脸书	臉書	liǎnshū	Facebook	n.	你用不用"脸书"？(Do you use "Facebook"?)

第二课 我们保持联络!
Lesson 2 Let's Keep in Touch!

29. 加入	加入	jiārù	to join	v.	加入我们吧。(Join us.)
30. 名单	名單	míngdān	list	n.	你的朋友名单中有一个人叫李小明。(There is a person called Li Xiaoming on your friend list.)
31. 邻居	鄰居	línjū	neighbor	n.	他是我以前的邻居。(He was my neighbor in the past.)
32. 巧	巧	qiǎo	such a coincidence		我刚做好饭你就来了,真巧!(The dinner is just ready and you come. What a coincidence!)
33. 想念	想念	xiǎngniàn	to miss someone	v.	我很想念你。(I miss you.)
34. 常常	常常	chángcháng	often	adv.	我们常常聊天。(We often chat.)
35. 保持	保持	bǎochí	to keep	v.	我们保持联络。(Let's keep in touch.)

专有名词 Proper Nouns

简体 (Simplified)	繁体 (Traditional)	拼音 (Pinyin)	释义 (Definition)	词性 (Parts of speech)	例句 (Examples)
1. 新墨西哥州	新墨西哥州	Xīnmòxīgē zhōu	New Mexico	p.n.	我要去新墨西哥州。(I want to go to New Mexico.)
2. 纽约	紐約	Niǔyuē	New York	p.n.	张爱友坐飞机回纽约 (Zhang Aiyou take a flight to return to New York)

补充词语 Supplementary Vocabulary

Simplified	Traditional	Pinyin	Definition
1. 笔友	筆友	bǐyǒu	pen pal (n.)

沟通任务 Communication Tasks

I) Indicating the method of transportation to go or return to a certain place

To go to a certain place...

我坐_____去_____。

(I take_____to go to_____.)

To return to a certain place...

我坐_____回_____。

(I take_____to return to_____.)

Examples:

我坐<u>公交车</u>去<u>学校</u>。

(I <u>take a bus</u> to <u>go to school</u>.)

我坐<u>飞机</u>回<u>新墨西哥州</u>。

(I take <u>a flight</u> to return to <u>New Mexico</u>.)

Practice: Tell a classmate sitting near you that you take the school bus to go to school and that you take a bus to return home.

II) Asking the question "why"

Question: 为什么_____?

          (Why_____?)

Answer: 因为_____。

         (Because_____.)

Examples:

Question: 为什么<u>你明天要回新墨西哥州</u>?

         (Why <u>do you want to return to New Mexico tomorrow?</u>)

Answer: 因为<u>我们学校后天开学</u>。

         (Because <u>school starts the day after tomorrow.</u>)

Question: 为什么<u>你不写作业</u>?

         (Why <u>don't you do your homework?</u>)

Answer: 因为<u>我早上写完了</u>。

Lesson 2 Let's Keep in Touch!
第二课 我们保持联络！

(Because I finished it in the morning.)

Practice: Work in pairs and think of a "why" question to ask each other. The person who answers the question needs to start the sentence with "因为".

III Asking if one can do something before leaving

Question: 你离开以前可以_____吗？

(Can you _____ before leaving?)

Answer: 当然可以。

(Of course I can.)

Or

当然没问题。

(Of course. No problem.)

Example:

Question: 你离开以前可以给我你的电子邮件地址吗？

(Can you give me your e-mail address before leaving?)

Answer: 当然可以。

(Of course I can.)

Or

当然没问题。

(Of course. No problem.)

Practice: Use the grammar structure, "你离开以前可以_____吗？" to ask a classmate a question.

IV Stating what you want to do after returning to a place

我回_____以后想_____。

(I want to_____ after I return to_____.)

Examples:

我回新墨西哥州以后想寄一张风景明信片给你。

(I want to send you a scenery postcard after I return to New Mexico.)

我回家以后想做作业。

(I want to do homework after I return home.)

Practice: What do you want to do after you return home today? Tell your classmates.

21

V. Suggesting to write certain information on a piece of paper

我们把_____写在一张纸上吧。

(Let's write_____on a piece of paper.)

Examples:

我们把<u>我们的电子邮件地址</u>写在一张纸上吧。

(Let's write <u>our e-mail addresses</u> on a piece of paper.)

我们把<u>我们的即时通讯账号</u>写在一张纸上吧。

(Let's write <u>our instant messenger account</u> on a piece of paper.)

我们把<u>我们的手机号码</u>写在一张纸上吧。

(Let's write <u>our cell phone numbers</u> on a piece of paper.)

我们把<u>地址</u>写在一张纸上吧。

(Let's write <u>our addresses</u> on a piece of paper.)

Practice: Suggest to a classmate to write his or her name on a piece of paper.

VI. Asking if one can see you on the computer

Question: 你在电脑上_____我吗?

(Can you see me on the computer?)

Positive Answer: 看得到。

(Yes, I can.)

Negative Answer: 看不到。

(No, I can't.)

Examples:

Question: 你在电脑上<u>看得到</u>我吗?

(Can you see me on the computer?)

Positive Answer: 看得到。

(Yes, I can.)

Negative Answer: 看不到。

(No, I can't.)

Elaborated Answer: 看不到,因为你还没安装网络摄像机。

(No, I can't because you haven't set up a webcam.)

Practice: Act out having an online chat with a classmate and ask each other if he or she can see you on the computer.

第二课　我们保持联络！
Lesson 2　Let's Keep in Touch!

VII Asking if one uses a certain thing

Question: 你用不用_____? / 你用_____吗?
(Do you use_____?)
Positive Answer: 用。
(Yes, I do.)
Negative Answer: 不用。
(No, I don't.)

Example:

Question: 你用不用"脸书"? / 你用"脸书"吗?
(Do you use "Facebook"?)
Positive Answer: 用。
(Yes, I do.)
Negative Answer: 不用。
(No, I don't.)

Practice: Ask your classmate if he or she uses the Chinese book.

VIII Stating that you know a person in someone's friend list on Facebook

Statement: 你的朋友名单中有一个人叫_____。他是我_____!
(There is a person named _____ on your friend list. He is my _____!)
Response: 真巧!
(What a coincidence!)

Example:

Statement: 你的朋友名单中有一个人叫<u>李小明</u>。他是我<u>以前的邻居</u>!
(There is a person named <u>李小明</u> on your friend list. He is my <u>former neighbor</u>.)
Response: 真巧!
(What a coincidence!)

Practice: Do you see anyone you know on your classmate's friend list on Facebook? Use the grammar structure taught above to tell the class who you recognized on the list.

IX) Stating your hope

希望_____。
(I hope _____.)

Example:

希望<u>我们能常常用即时通讯聊天</u>。
(I hope <u>we can often use instant messenger to chat.</u>)

Practice: Tell your class what you hope to do with them in class.

情景（一）Scenario 1

去年暑假张爱华去加州看他亲戚时遇到了一个新的中国朋友李大鹏。

李大鹏： 爱华，明天你要不要跟我一起溜滑板？

张爱华： 对不起，我明天不能跟你一起溜滑板。我明天早上八点得坐飞机回新墨西哥州。

李大鹏： 为什么你明天要回新墨西哥州？

张爱华： 因为我们学校后天开学。我得回学校上课。你呢？你们学校什么时候开学？

李大鹏： 我们学校下星期才开学。

张爱华： 真棒！

李大鹏： 你离开以前可以给我你的电子邮件地址吗？我想给你写邮件。

张爱华： 当然可以。我们也可以用即时通讯联络。

李大鹏： 好啊。我还想打电话给你。你可以给我你的手机号码吗？

张爱华： 当然没问题。我回新墨西哥州以后想寄一张风景明信片给你，你可以给我你的地址吗？

李大鹏： 可以啊。我们把电子邮件地址、即时通讯地址、手机号码和收信地址写在一张纸上吧。

Comprehension Questions

1. 张爱华为什么要回新墨西哥州？
2. 李大鹏的学校什么时候开学？
3. 张爱华回新墨西哥州以后想做什么？

情景（二）Scenario 2

张爱华和李大鹏正在即时通上聊天。

张爱华： 大鹏，你在电脑上看得到我吗？

Lesson 2　Let's Keep in Touch!
第二课　我们保持联络！

李大鹏： 我看不到你，因为你还没安装网络摄像机。

张爱华： 你用不用"脸书"？

李大鹏： 用啊。

张爱华： 加入我的朋友名单吧。我想给你看我的新照片。

李大鹏把张爱华加到"脸书"的朋友名单里。

李大鹏： 你的朋友名单中有一个人叫李小明。他是我以前的邻居！

张爱华： 真巧！

Comprehension Questions

1. 为什么李大鹏在电脑上看不到张爱华？
2. 李大鹏用不用"脸书"？

情景（三）Scenario 3

李大鹏收到了张爱华的明信片。

亲爱的大鹏：
　　好久不见！你好吗？你还是每天溜滑板吗？你们学校开学了吗？
　　我很想念你。希望我们能常常用即时通讯聊天。
　　保持联络！

　　　　　　　　　　　　　　　　　　　　　　　　　　　张爱华

Comprehension Questions

1. 张爱华想念李大鹏吗？
2. 张爱华想用什么跟李大鹏聊天？

口语沟通活动 Oral Communication Activities

I. 情况：林丽想找个朋友跟她去逛街，但是她的朋友们明天都有事（他们明天的计划在下方）。

Situation: Lin Li wants to find a friend to go shopping with her tomorrow, but it seems that her friends all have plans for tomorrow (see their plans below).

Lin Li's friends	Things they plan to do	Reasons
陈林	坐火车去加州	我奶奶生日
王文丽	坐出租车去中国饭馆	见我的笔友（pen pal）
林强	坐飞机去中国	旅行
张爱友	坐飞机回纽约	看我爸爸妈妈

任务：两人一组。一个人扮演林丽，另一个人扮演林丽的朋友。林丽需要用下方的会话结构来邀她的朋友一起逛街。林丽的朋友需要用上方表格内的资讯来告诉林丽为什么他不能跟她一起去逛街。

Task: Work in pairs. One acts as Lin Li and the other acts as Lin Li's friends. Linli needs to use the following conversation structure to ask her friends to go shopping. Lin Li's friends need to use the information provided above to tell Lin Li why they can't go with her to shop tomorrow.

会话结构：

Conversation structure

林丽：明天你要不要跟我一起去逛街？
陈林：对不起，我明天不能跟你一起去逛街。我明天得坐火车去加州。
林丽：为什么你明天要坐火车去加州？
陈林：因为我奶奶生日。

II. 情况：你想知道班上有几个人使用电邮、即时通讯、脸书和手机。

Situation: You are curious about how many people in class use e-mail, instant messenger, Facebook, or a cell phone.

任务：用下方的会话结构问十个同学他们使用上述的哪几项。在下方表格写下他们的名字并勾选他们的答案。

Task: Use the conversation structure listed below to survey at least 10 classmates about their use of the technology mentioned above. Write down their names in the

Lesson 2 Let's Keep in Touch!

table below and put a check mark under the type of technology they use.

会话结构：

Conversation structure:

你：你用不用电子邮件？

你的同学：用。

你的同学：不用。

姓名	电子邮件	即时通讯	"脸书"	手机
1.				
2.				
3.				
4.				
5.				
6.				
7.				
8.				
9.				
10.				

你问过的同学当中有几个人使用电子邮件、即时通讯、"脸书"和手机？在下方表格里写下人数并用以下句型做课堂报告："__个人用电子邮件，"__个人用即时通讯，"__个人用脸书，"__个人用手机"。

How many people you surveyed used 电子邮件, 即时通讯, "脸书", or 手机? Write down the numbers in the table below and report them to the class using the sentence structure, "个人用电子邮件,"个人用即时通讯,"个人用脸书,"个人用手机".

	电子邮件	即时通讯	脸书	手机
人数 # of people				

读写沟通活动 Literacy Communication Activities

1. 陈文丽在他朋友"脸书"上的朋友名单看到了许多熟悉的面孔。她想在及时通讯上告诉她朋友她在"脸书"看到了什么,但是她有些汉字忘了怎么写。你的任务是帮陈文丽和她的朋友们完成下方及时通的对话。

Chen Wenli was browsing through her friends' friend lists on Facebook and saw many familiar faces. She wants to tell her friends on instant messenger about what she saw in the friend lists, but forgot how to write some of the Chinese words. Your task is to help Chen Wenli and her friends to complete the written conversation in Chinese.

陈文丽和陈美的对话　Chen Wenli and Chen Mei's conversation

> 陈文丽:你的朋友名单中有一个人叫李大明。他是_____!
> 　　　　　　　　　　　　　　　　　　　(my former manager)
>
> 陈　美:_____!
> 　　　(What a coincidence!)

陈文丽和王兴的对话　Chen Wenli and Wang Xing's conversation

> 陈文丽:你的朋友名单中有一个人叫陈林。他是_____!
> 　　　　　　　　　　　　　　　　　　(my former classmate)
>
> 王　兴:_____!
> 　　　(What a coincidence!)

陈文丽和吴真的对话　Chen Wenli and Wu Zhen's conversation

> 陈文丽:_____叫小红。她是_____!
> 　　　(There is a person named Xiao Hong on your friend list.) (my former teacher)
>
> 吴　真:_____!
> 　　　(What a coincidence!)

Lesson 2 Let's Keep in Touch!
第二课 我们保持联络!

陈文丽和林丽的对话   Chen Wenli and Lin Li's conversation

陈文丽：_____叫王文中。
(There is a person named Wang Wenzhong on your friend list.)
他是_____！
(my former neighbor)
林　丽：_____！
(What a coincidence!)

II. 陈林和一个明天将要回中国的朋友张安在网上聊天。有些词和短语陈林和张安没办法用中文打。帮助他们完成下列对话。
Chen Lin is chatting on-line with a friend who is going to return to China tomorrow. There are words and phrases Chen Lin and Zhang An are unable to type in Chinese. Help them complete the conversation in the blanks below.

张安：你在电脑上_____我吗?
(Can you see me on the computer?)
陈林：_____。_____?
　　　(Yes, I can.)   (How are you today?)
张安：_____因为我明天要_____。
(I am very happy today because I am going to return to China tomorrow.)
陈林：真_____！你_____以前可以给我_____吗?
　　　(Wonderful!)　(Can you give me your cell phone number before leaving?)
张安：_____。我回_____以后想寄_____给你。
　　　(Of course I can.)   (I want to send you a postcard after I return to China.)
陈林：_____！_____！
　　　(Thank you!)   (Let's keep in touch!)
张安：希望我们能常常_____聊天。
(I hope we can often use cell phones to chat.)

讨论 Discussion

Internet Usage in China

According to a report published by China Internet Network Information Center (CNNIC), China had 420 million Internet users by June 2010. The Data Center of China Internet (DCCI) predicts that China's Internet population will hit 718 million by 2013, accounting for 52.7 percent of the total population in China. In the latest estimates for Internet users by language presented by Internet World Stats, Chinese language is the number 2 language on the web. There are several websites that Chinese speakers use:

1. 百度(Bǎidù) is the leading search engine. 百度 offers several services to locate information, products and services using Chinese language.

2. Sina (Xīnlàng) is a multiple-service provider. Its major services are SMS, e-mail, search, games, entertainment, and blogs.

3. QQ is the most popular free instant messaging program in China.

Discussion Question:
1. Try 百度, Sina, and QQ. What features do you like/dislike?

Reference:
X. Qiang (2010) User-generated content online now 50.7% of total. *China Daily*. Retrieved September 10, 2011 from the World Wide Web: http://www.chinadaily.com.cn/bizchina/2010-07/23/content_11042851.htm

Lesson 3

你们准备好点菜了吗?
Are You Ready to Order?

沟通任务 Communication Tasks

- Waiter or waitress asking how many people are in the group and leading them to a table.
- Waiter or waitress asking customers if they would like to sit at a certain table.
- Waiter or waitress asking if customers are ready to order.
- Asking what today's special is.
- Asking what one wants to order.
- Waiter or waitress asking if customers need drinks.
- Stating that you can't finish the meal and need it to go.
- Offering to treat someone.

课前讨论 Warm-up Discussion Questions

1. Do you often go to eat in a restaurant with your friends?
2. Is there a preferred space you usually like to sit in a restaurant?
3. If you can't finish your meal, do you usually ask for a to-go box?

生词 Vocabulary

简体 (Simplified)	繁体 (Traditional)	拼音 (Pinyin)	释义 (Definition)	词性 (Parts of speech)	例句 (Examples)
1. 服务员	服務員	fúwùyuán	service personnel	n.	他是一个餐厅服务员。(He is a restaurant waiter.)
2. 欢迎光临	歡迎光臨	huānyíng guānglín	welcome		欢迎光临! (Welcome!)
3. 几	幾	jǐ	how many	pron.	
位	位	wèi	classifier for persons	m.w.	请问几位？(How many [people]?)
4. 这边	這邊	zhè biān	this way		爷爷, 这边请。(This way please, grandfather.)
5. 座位	座位	zuòwèi	seat	n.	我想坐这个座位。(I want to sit in this seat.)
6. 可以	可以	kěyǐ	can	aux.	我可以坐这个座位吗？(Can I sit in this seat?)
7. 这	這	zhè	this	pron.	这是你的书。(This is your book.)
8. 菜单	菜單	càidān	menu	n.	这是菜单。(This is the menu.)
9. 慢慢	慢慢	mànman	slowly	adj.	请慢慢看。(Please take your time to read.)
10. 准备	準備	zhǔnbèi	to prepare	v.	你准备好了吗？(Are you ready?)
11. 点菜	點菜	diǎn cài	to order food	v.o.	我妈妈想点菜。(My mother wants to order food.)
12. 一点	一點	yìdiǎn	a little	nm.	我还需要一点水。(I still need a little more water.)
13. 没问题	沒問題	méi wèntí	no problem		没问题。(No problem.)
14. 特色菜	特色菜	tèsècài	special dish	n.	今天的特色菜是什么？(What is today's special?)
15. 烤羊排	烤羊排	kǎoyángpái	roasted lamb chop		我想吃烤羊排。(I want to eat roasted lamb chops.)
16. 份	份	fèn	(an) order	m.w.	我要点一份烤羊排。(I would like an order of the roasted lamb chops.)

第三课 你们准备好点菜了吗?
Lesson 3 Are You Ready to Order?

17. 招牌菜	招牌菜	zhāopái cài	signature dish; a dish that a restaurant is well known for	n.	我们的招牌菜是烤羊排。(Our signature dish is roasted lamb chops.)
18. 炖牛肉	燉牛肉	dùnniúròu	beef stew		我要一份炖牛肉。(I want an order of beef stew.)
19. 吃素	吃素	chīsù	to be a vegetarian	v.	我吃素。(I am a vegetarian.)
20. 杯	杯	bēi	a classifier for cups/glasses	m.w.	我想喝一杯茶。(I want to drink a cup of tea.)
21. 好了	好了	hǎo le	I am fine with just...		我喝水就好了。(I am fine with just water.)
22. 马上	馬上	mǎshàng	immediately	adv.	好,我马上来。(Okay, I will come immediately.)
23. 完	完	wán	to finish	v.	我吃不完。(I can't finish eating.)
24. 打包	打包	dǎ bāo	to pack up	v.o.	我要打包。(I want to pack.)
25. 带走	帶走	dàizǒu	to take away		我要打包带走。(I want to wrap it up and take it.)
26. 盒子	盒子	hézi	box	n.	请给我一个盒子。(Please give me a box.)
27. 账单	賬單	zhàngdān	bill	n.	这是你们的帐单。(This is your bill.)
28. 请客	請客	qǐng kè	to treat someone to a meal		今天我请客。(It's on me today.)
29. 不好意思	不好意思	bù hǎoyìsi	embarrassed		真不好意思!(I am really embarrassed!)

补充词语 Supplementary Vocabulary

Simplified	Traditional	Pinyin	Definition
1. 用	用	yòng	to use; to need (v.)
2. 那边	那邊	nà biān	over there (pron.)
3. 角落	角落	jiǎoluò	corner (n.)
4. 门	門	mén	door (n.)
5. 柱子	柱子	zhùzi	post (n.)

沟通任务 Communication Tasks

I. Waiter or waitress asking how many people are in the group and leading them to a table

Waiter or Waitress: 欢迎光临。请问几位？
          (Welcome. How many?)

Customer: _____ 位。
       (_____.)

Waiter or Waitress: 这边请。
          (This way please.)

Example:

Waiter or Waitress: 欢迎光临。请问几位？
          (Welcome. How many?)

Customer: 三位。
       (Three.)

Waiter or Waitress: 这边请。
          (This way please.)

Practice: Work in groups of 3 to 4. One acts as a waiter or waitress, and the rest act as customers. Use the sentence structure introduced above to make a conversation.

II. Waiter or waitress asking customers if they would like to sit at a certain table

Waiter or Waitress: 请问这个座位可以吗？
          (How about this table?)

Positive Answer: 可以,谢谢。
          (Great, thanks.)

Negative Answer: 我可以坐_____吗？
          (Can I sit _____?)

Example:

Waiter or Waitress: 请问这个座位可以吗？
(How about this table?)
Positive Answer: 可以，谢谢。
(Great, thanks.)
Negative Answer 1: 我可以坐那边吗？
(Can I sit over there?)
Negative Answer 2: 我可以坐窗户旁边吗？
(Can I sit by the window?)

Practice: Continue the role play in Communication Tasks Practice I. The waiter or waitress asks the customers if they like the place they are going to sit. The customers are free to decide to give a positive or negative answer.

III Waiter or Waitress asking if customers are ready to order

Waiter or Waitress: 请问你们准备好点菜了吗？
(Are you ready to order?)
Positive Answer: 好了。
(Ready.)
Negative Answer: 还没，我们还需要一点时间。
(Not yet, we still need a little more time.)

Practice: Continue the role play in Communication Tasks Practice II. The waiter or waitress asks the customer, "Are you ready to order?", and the customers answer, "Not yet, we still need a little more time.". The waiter or waitress asks the same question again, and this time the customers give a positive answer.

IV Asking what today's special is

Customer: 请问今天的特色菜是什么？
(What's today's special?)
Waiter/Waitress: 今天的特色菜是_____。
(Today's special is_____.)

Example:

Customer: 请问今天的特色菜是什么？
(What's today's special?)

Waiter/Waitress: 今天的特色菜是<u>烤羊排</u>。

(Today's special is <u>roasted lamb chops</u>.)

Practice: Continue the role play in Communication Tasks Practice III. The customers ask what today's special is and the waiter or waitress needs to answer, "Today's special is beef hamburger.".

V Asking what one wants to order

Question: 你要点什么？

(What do you want to order?)

Answer: 我要(点)_____。

(I want (to order) _____.)

Example:

Question: 你要点什么？

(What do you want to order?)

Answer 1: 我要<u>一份烤羊排</u>。

(I want <u>an order of roasted lamb chops</u>.)

Answer 2: 我要点<u>招牌菜——炖牛肉</u>。

(I want to order <u>the signature dish—beef stew</u>.)

Answer 3: 我要点<u>一份蔬菜沙拉</u>。

(I want to order <u>a vegetable salad.</u>)

Practice: Continue the role play in Communication Tasks Practice IV. The waiter or waitress asks what the customers want to order. Each of the customers thinks of a dish to order.

VI Waiter or waitress asking if customers need drinks

Question: 请问你(们)需要饮料吗？

(Do you need drinks?)

Answer: 我_____。

(I_____.)

Example:

Question: 请问你(们)需要饮料吗？

(Do you need drinks?)

Lesson 3 Are You Ready to Order?
第三课 你们准备好点菜了吗？

Answer 1: 我<u>要一杯汽水</u>。
(I <u>want a glass of soda</u>.)

Answer 2: 我<u>也是</u>。
(<u>So do</u> I.)

Answer 3: 我<u>喝水就好了</u>。
(<u>I am fine with just water.</u>)

Practice: Continue the role play in Communication Tasks Practice V. The waiter or waitress asks if the customers need drinks, and each of the customers orders a drink of their choice.

VII) Stating that you can't finish the meal and need it to go

我吃不完我的_____。我要打包带走。
(I can't finish my _____. I want to wrap it up and take it.)

Examples:

我吃不完我的<u>菜</u>。我要打包带走。
(I can't finish my <u>dish</u>. I want to wrap it up and take it.)

我吃不完我的<u>沙拉</u>。我要打包带走。
(I can't finish my <u>salad</u>. I want to wrap it up and take it.)

Practice: Continue the role play in Communication Tasks Practice VI. The customers need to tell the waiter or waitress that they can't finish their dishes and that they want to wrap it up and take it.

VIII) Offering to treat someone

Statement: 我请客。
(It's on me.)

Accepting the offer: 真不好意思。谢谢你。
(I am embarrassed. Thank you.)

Rejecting the offer: 真不好意思。不用[yòng]了。
(I am embarrassed. You don't need to do that.)

Practice: Continue the role play in Communication Tasks Practice VII. One of the customers tells the rest, "It's on me", and the rest of the customers accept the offer by saying, "I am embarrassed. Thank you."

情景(一) Scenario 1

李小明、张爱华和吴家玲正要去饭馆庆祝李小明的生日。

服务员：欢迎光临。请问几位？
李小明：三位。
服务员：这边请。

服务员带客人到他们的桌子……

服务员：请问这个座位可以吗？
李小明：可以，谢谢。
服务员：这是菜单。请慢慢看。

五分钟后……

服务员：请问你们准备好点菜了吗？
张爱华：我们还需要一点时间。
服务员：没问题。

五分钟后……

吴家玲：请问今天的特色菜是什么？
服务员：今天的特色菜是烤羊排。
吴家玲：我要点一份烤羊排。小明、爱华，你们要点什么？
李小明：我要点招牌菜——炖牛肉。
张爱华：我吃素，所以我要点一份蔬菜沙拉。
服务员：请问你们需要饮料吗？
吴家玲：我要一杯汽水。
李小明：我也是。
张爱华：我喝水就好了。
服务员：好，马上来。

Comprehension Questions

1. 今天的特色菜是什么？
2. 李小明点了什么？
3. 吴家玲点了什么？
4. 张爱华要喝什么？

第三课 你们准备好点菜了吗?
Lesson 3 Are You Ready to Order?

情景(二) Scenario 2

李小明、张爱华和吴家玲吃完了……

李小明: 服务员,我吃不完我的菜。我要打包带走。
服务员: 好。我给你一个盒子。

两分钟后……

服务员: 这是你们的账单。
李小明: 爱华、家玲,谢谢你们跟我一起庆祝我的生日。今天我请客。
张爱华和吴家玲: 真不好意思。谢谢你!

Comprehension Questions

1. 谁想打包带走?
2. 谁请客?

情景(三) Scenario 3

李小明正在写他的日记……

李小明的日记

今天是我的生日,我和朋友们一起去了餐厅吃饭,我请客。朋友们,谢谢你们和我一起庆祝生日。

李小明

Comprehension Questions

1. 今天李小明和谁庆祝生日?
2. 为什么李小明要谢谢他的朋友们?

口语沟通活动 Oral Communication Activities

I. 情况：陈林是一家饭馆的服务员。今晚他要服务六组的客人。下表提供了这六组客人的人数和他们喜欢的座位。

Situation: Chen Lin works as a waiter in a restaurant. He is going to serve 6 groups of people this evening. The table below provides the information about the number of people in each group and their preferred seats.

客人	人数	喜欢的座位
第一组	三位	角落 (corner)
第二组	五位	窗户旁边
第三组	两位	门 (door) 旁边
第四组	一位	柱子 (post) 后面
第五组	一位	柱子前面
第六组	两位	无特定喜欢的座位

任务：分小组练习。一个人扮演陈林，其他人扮演客人。陈林可以用下方的会话结构带客人到他们喜欢的座位。

Task: Work in small groups. One acts as Chen Lin and the rest act as customer groups. Chen Lin needs to use the following conversation structure to lead the customers to their preferred seats.

会话结构：

Conversation Structure:

陈林：欢迎光临。请问几位？

第一组客人：<u>三位</u>。

陈林：这边请。

（陈林带客人到他们的座位。）

陈林：请问这个座位可以吗？

第一组客人：我们可以坐<u>角落</u>吗？

陈林：没问题。这边请。

（陈林带客人到他们喜欢的座位。）

第三课 你们准备好点菜了吗?
Lesson 3 Are You Ready to Order?

II. 情况:陈林正在服务第二组的五个客人。下方列出了这五个客人要点的菜和饮料。

Situation: Chen Lin is serving the 5 customers in Group 2. The dishes and drinks the 5 customers are going to order are listed below.

客人	菜	饮料
客人一	烤羊排	咖啡
客人二	猪肉汉堡	可口可乐
客人三	水果沙拉	冰茶
客人四	鸡肉炒饭	水
客人五	牛肉面	果汁

任务:分小组练习。一个人扮演陈林,其他人扮演客人。陈林需要用下方的会话结构来帮客人点菜。

Task: Work in small groups. One acts as Chen Lin and the rest act as the customers. Chen Lin needs to follow the conversation structure below to help the customers place their orders.

会话结构:
Conversation Structure:
陈林: 请问你准备好点菜了吗?
客人一: 好了。
陈林: 你要点什么?
客人一: 我要点<u>一份烤羊排</u>。
陈林: 请问你需要饮料吗?
客人一: 我要<u>一杯咖啡</u>。

读写沟通活动 Literacy Communication Activities

1. 陈文丽在决定今晚去哪家饭馆前,想先打电话到她最喜欢的三家饭馆问问他们今日的特色菜和招牌菜是什么。帮助陈文丽在下面写下饭馆的答案。

Chen Wenli wants to call her three favorite restaurants to find out the signature dishes and today's specials before deciding which restaurant to go to this evening. Help Chen Wenli write notes about the dishes offered in the three restaurants in the blanks under the pictures below.

(1) 第一家饭馆
　　招牌菜:_____(Our signature dish is beef hamburger.)
　　今天的特别菜:_____(Today's special is chicken hamburger.)

(2) 第二家饭馆
　　招牌菜:_____(Our signature dish is beef stew.)
　　今天的特色菜:_____(Today's special is roasted lamb chops.)

(3) 第三家饭馆
　　招牌菜:_____(Our signature dish is stir fry noodles.)
　　今天的特色菜:_____(Today's special is fried rice.)

第三课 你们准备好点菜了吗?
Lesson 3 Are You Ready to Order?

II. 昨天是林强的生日。他收到了很多朋友送他的礼物。为了感谢他的朋友们,林强想请他们到中国饭馆吃饭。林强传了一个短信给他的朋友们。一些朋友们接受、一些朋友们回绝了他的邀请。林强的朋友们用英文回答。找一个同学一起把英文翻译成中文。

Yesterday was Lin Qiang's birthday. He received many gifts from his friends. In order to thank his friends, Lin Qiang wants to treat them to a nice meal at a Chinese restaurant. Lin Qiang sent an invitation text message to his friends. Some of his friends accepted and some declined. The conversation is already written in English. Work with a classmate and translate the conversation into Chinese.

陈林的手机
Chen Lin's cell phone

林强: 今天我们一起去中国饭馆吃饭好不好?

陈林: _____
(Sure.)

林强: 今天我请客。

陈林: _____
(I am really embarrassed. Thanks.)

林美的手机
Lin Mei's cell phone

林强: 今天我们一起去中国饭馆吃饭好不好?

林美: _____
(Sure.)

林强: 今天我请客。

林美: _____
(I am really embarrassed. You don't need to do that.)

43

吴家玲的手机
Wu Jialing's cell phone

林强: 今天我们一起去中国饭馆吃饭好不好?

吴家玲: _____
(Sorry, but I need to go to the Chinese class today.)

讨论 Discussion

Chinese Dining Etiquette

Chinese dining etiquette is distinctive from western etiquette. At meal times, Chinese people usually use a round table. The use of a round table has a cultural meaning for the Chinese as 圆 (yuán, roundedness) symbolizes reunion as exhibited by the word 团圆 (tuányuán, reunion). Unlike westerners who use forks and knives to dine, Chinese people use a pair of chopsticks and spoons.

There are several things to remember when you dine in Chinese style:

1. Chinese people pay high respect to the elders, teachers, and guests; therefore, one should not start to eat until the elders, teachers, or the guests have started eating.

2. Avoid resting chopsticks vertically in a bowl as it resembles the incense sticks that the Chinese traditionally burn in respect of deceased loved ones.

3. It is a tradition to pour tea for others. Members of a dinner party will regularly refill the cups of those around them.

Lesson 3 Are You Ready to Order?
第三课 你们准备好点菜了吗？

Discussion Question:

1. Get into small groups and role play dining in Chinese style. Your teacher will observe if you show adequate Chinese dining etiquette.

第四课
Lesson 4

我迷路了
I am Lost on the Road

沟通任务 Communication Tasks

- Asking for directions.
- Asking which floor one is going to.
- Questioning why one arrives late.
- Suggesting that one stops and asks for directions.

课前讨论 Warm-up Discussion Questions

1. Have you been lost on the way to an important event? What do you usually do when you are lost?

生词 Vocabulary

简体 (Simplified)	繁体 (Traditional)	拼音 (Pinyin)	释义 (Definition)	词性 (Parts of speech)	例句 (Examples)
1. 地铁站	地鐵站	dìtiězhàn	subway station	n.	地铁站在哪儿？(Where is the subway station?)

Lesson 4 I am Lost on the Road
第四课 我迷路了

2. 这里	這裡	zhèlǐ	here	*pron.*	来这里。(Come here.)
3. 直走	直走	zhí zǒu	go straight		请直走。(Please go straight.)
4. 过	過	guò	to pass	*v.*	过了学校以后你会看到中国饭馆。(You will see the Chinese restaurant after passing the school.)
5. 红绿灯	紅綠燈	hónglǜdēng	traffic light	*n.*	过了三个红绿灯以后你会看到地铁站。(After passing three traffic lights, you will see the subway station.)
6. 右转	右轉	yòu zhuǎn	to turn right		请右转。(Please turn right.)
7. 就	就	jiù	right away	*adv.*	右转就到了。(You will arrive right away if you take a right.)
8. 警卫	警衛	jǐngwèi	security guard	*n.*	我问警卫先生一个问题。(I ask the security guard a question.)
9. 电梯	電梯	diàntī	elevator	*n.*	电梯在哪儿？(Where is the elevator?)
10. 往	往	wǎng	toward	*prep.*	往中山路直走就到了。(You will arrive right away if you go straight toward Zhongshang road.)
11. 大厅	大廳	dàtīng	hall	*n.*	往大厅直走就到了。(You will arrive right away if you go straight toward the hall.)
12. 雕像	雕像	diāoxiàng	statue	*n.*	维纳斯雕像很漂亮。(The Venus statue is pretty.)
13. 左转	左轉	zuǒ zhuǎn	to turn left		请在这里左转。(Please take a left here.)
14. 这么	這麼	zhème	so	*pron.*	你怎么这么早到？(How come you arrived so early?)
15. 晚	晚	wǎn	to be late	*adj.*	你怎么这么晚到？(How come you arrived so late?)
16. 迷路	迷路	mí lù	to get lost on the road		我迷路了！(I am lost on the road!)

47

17. 欢送会	歡送會	huānsòng huì	farewell party	n.	今天晚上我参加了我朋友的欢送会。(I joined my friend's farewell party this evening.)
18. 停	停	tíng	to stop	v.	停下来！(Stop!)
19. 间	間	jiān	classifier for rooms and buildings	m.w.	这间学校很大。(This school is very big.)
20. 加油站	加油站	jiāyóuzhàn	gas station	n.	这间加油站的服务员很好。(The service staff in this gas station is very nice.)
21. 体育场	體育場	tǐyùchǎng	stadium	n.	体育场在哪儿？(Where is the stadium?)
22. 高速公路	高速公路	gāosù gōnglù	freeway		二十八号高速公路怎么走？(How do you get to freeway 28?)
23. 出口	出口	chūkǒu	exit	n.	五号出口在哪儿？(Where is exit 5?)
24. 下来	下來	xiàlái	to get off	v.	下来！(Get off!)
25. 掉头	掉頭	diào tuó	to make an U-turn		这里不可以掉头。(One cannot make an U-turn here.)
26. 找不到	找不到	zhǎo bú dào	cannot find		我找不到地铁站。(I cannot find the subway station.)
27. 摩天大楼	摩天大樓	mótiāndàlóu	skyscraper		纽约有很多摩天大楼。(New York has many skyscrapers.)
28. 告诉	告訴	gàosu	to tell	v.	警卫先生告诉我动物园怎么走。(The security guard told me how to get to the zoo.)
29. 找到	找到	zhǎodào	to find		我找到了。(I found it!)
30. 终于	終於	zhōngyú	eventually; finally	adv.	我终于找到了。(I finally found it!)

第四课 我迷路了
Lesson 4 I am Lost on the Road

专有名词 Proper Nouns

简体 (Simplified)	繁体 (Traditional)	拼音 (Pinyin)	释义 (Definition)	词性 (Parts of speech)	例句 (Examples)
1. 维纳斯	維納斯	Wéinàsī	Venus	n.	维纳斯很漂亮。(Venus is pretty.)
2. 中央公园	中央公園	Zhōngyāng gōngyuán	Central Park	p.n.	这个公园叫中央公园。(This park is called Central Park)
3. 犹他大学	猶他大學	Yóutā dàxué	University of Utah	p.n.	犹他大学在盐湖城。(University of Utah is in Salt Lake City)

补充词语 Supplementary Vocabulary

Simplified	Traditional	Pinyin	Definition
1. 动物园	動物園	dòngwùyuán	zoo (n.)
2. 博物馆	博物館	bówùguǎn	museum (n.)
3. 美术馆	美術館	měishùguǎn	art museum (n.)
4. 火车站	火車站	huǒchēzhàn	train station (n.)
5. 水族馆	水族館	shuǐzúguǎn	aquarium (n.)
6. 中国城	中國城	Zhōngguóchéng	Chinatown (n.)
7. 警察	警察	jǐngchá	police (n.)
8. 司机	司機	sījī	driver (n.)
9. 校长室	校長室	xiàozhǎngshì	Principal's office (n.)
10. 学生食堂	學生食堂	xuéshēng shítáng	student cafeteria
11. 厕所	廁所	cèsuǒ	bathroom (n.)

沟通任务 Communication Tasks

I) Asking for directions (sentence structure 1)

Question: 你知不知道_____怎么走?

(Do you know how to get to_____?)

Positive answer: 知道。_____就到了。

(Yes, I do. You will arrive if you _____.)

Negative answer: 对不起,我不知道。

(Sorry, I don't know.)

Example:

Question: 你知不知道中山地铁站怎么走?

(Do you know how to get to the 中山 subway station?)

Positive answer: 知道。从这里直走就到了。

(Yes, I do. You will arrive if you go straight from here.)

Negative answer: 对不起,我不知道。

(Sorry, I don't know.)

Practice: Think of a place and ask if your classmate knows how to get there.

II) Asking for directions (sentence structure 2)

Question: 请问_____怎么走?

(How do you get to _____?)

Answer: _____就到了。

(You will arrive if you _____.)

Example:

Question: 请问中山地铁站怎么走?

(How do you get to the 中山 subway station?)

Answer: 从这里直走就到了。

(You will arrive if you go straight from here.)

Elaborated Answer: 从这里直走。过三个红绿灯以后右转就到了。

(Go straight from here. You will arrive if you take a right after passing three traffic lights.)

Question: 请问体育场怎么走?

Lesson 4 I am Lost on the Road
第四课 我迷路了

(How do you get to the stadium?)

Elaborated Answer: 你先上28号高速公路。在5号出口下来以后再掉头就到了。

(First get on freeway #28. You will arrive if you make an U-turn after you get off at Exit #5.)

Practice: Ask your classmate the directions to a certain place.

III Asking for directions (sentence structure 3)

Question: 请问 _____ 在哪儿？

(Where is _____ ?)

Answer: _____ 就到了。

(You will arrive if _____.)

Example:

Question: 请问电梯在哪儿？

(Where is the elevator?)

Elaborated Answer: 往大厅直走。看到维纳斯雕像以后左转就到了。

(Go straight toward the lobby. You will arrive if you take a left after you see the Venus statue.)

Practice: Ask your classmate where the Chinese classroom is.

IV Asking which floor one is going to

Question: 请问到几楼？

(Which floor?)

Answer：_____ 楼。

(_____ floor.)

Example:

Question: 请问到几楼？

(Which floor?)

Answer：56楼。

(The 56th floor.)

Practice: You and your classmate are in an elevator now. Ask each other which floor he or she is going to.

V) Questioning why one arrives late

Question: _____怎么这么晚到？
　　　　　(How come _____ arrived so late?)
Answer：对不起，_____！
　　　　　(Sorry, _____.)

Example:

Question: 你怎么这么晚到？
　　　　　(How come you arrived so late?)
Answer：对不起，我迷路了！
　　　　　(Sorry, I was lost on the road.)

Practice: Did any of your classmates arrive late today? Ask him or her the reason for arriving late.

VI) Suggesting that one stops and asks for directions

我们停下来问_____ _____怎么走吧。
(Let's stop and ask _____ how to get to _____.)

Example:

我们停下来问这间加油站的服务员 体育场怎么走吧。
(Let's stop and ask the staff in this gas station how to get to the stadium.)

Practice: You and your classmates are on the way to the zoo 动物园 [dòngwùyuán], but are lost. Suggest to each other in Chinese, "Let's stop and ask the passerby how to get to the zoo".

情景（一） Scenario 1

李小明的朋友沈心宜要去留学。沈心宜在摩天大楼办了一个欢送会。李小明想坐地铁去欢送会，但是他在途中迷路了。李小明正在打电话给他的朋友张爱华求救。

李小明：喂？请问爱华在吗？
张爱华：我就是。
李小明：我是小明。你知不知道中山地铁站怎么走？
张爱华：对不起，我不知道。你问别人吧。

李小明正找行人问地铁怎么走。

李小明：先生，请问中山地铁站怎么走？

第四课　我迷路了
Lesson 4　I am Lost on the Road

路　　人： 从这里直走。过三个红绿灯以后右转就到了。
李小明： 谢谢！

李小明终于到了摩天大楼,但是他找不到一楼的电梯。他决定问保安。

李 小 明： 警卫先生,请问电梯在哪儿?
警卫先生： 往大厅直走。看到维纳斯雕像以后左转就到了。
李 小 明： 谢谢！

李小明走进电梯里……

电梯小姐： 请问到几楼?
李 小 明： 56楼。谢谢。

李小明终于到了欢送会……

沈心宜： 小明,你怎么这么晚到?
李小明： 对不起,我迷路了！
沈心宜： 没关系。欢迎来我的欢送会。

Comprehension Questions

1. 张爱华知道中山地铁站怎么走吗?
2. 沈心宜的欢送会在几楼?
3. 李小明为什么晚到?

情景(二) Scenario 2

张爱华和他爸爸要去看一场棒球赛,但是他们在开车到体育场的途中迷路了。

爸爸： 我们停下来问这间加油站的服务员体育场怎么走吧。

张爱华下车向加油站服务员问路。

张爱华： 请问体育场怎么走?
服务员： 你先上28号高速公路。在5号出口下来以后再掉头就到了。
张爱华： 谢谢！

Comprehension Questions

1. 爸爸的车在哪儿停下来?

2. 张爱华和爸爸得上几号高速公路?

情景(三)Scenario 3

李小明正在写他的日记……

李小明的日记

今天晚上我参加了沈心宜的欢送会,但是我迷路了。我找不到中山地铁站。我也找不到摩天大楼的电梯。行人和警卫先生告诉我怎么走。最后我终于找到了,但是我也迟到了!

Comprehension Questions

1. 李小明向谁问路了?
2. 最后李小明找到要去的地方了吗?

口语沟通活动 Oral Communication Activities

I. 情况:林强在市中心散步时有几个行人因为迷路了而在向他问路。下方表格显示了每个行人想去的地点和走的方向。

Situation: Several passersby are lost and ask Lin Qiang for directions while he is taking a walk in the downtown area. The table below shows the place each passerby wants to go and the direction to each place from the current location.

行人	地点	怎么走
行人一	中央公园(Central Park)	从这里直走
行人二	动物园(zoo)	先过一个红绿灯再直走
行人三	博物馆(museum)	从这里左转
行人四	美术馆(art museum)	从这里右转
行人五	火车站(train station)	先从这里左转再直走
行人六	犹他大学(University of Utah)	先过两个红绿灯再右转

任务:两人一组。一个人扮演林强,另一个人扮演行人。用下方会话结构和上表资讯做角色扮演。

第四课 我迷路了
Lesson 4 I am Lost on the Road

Task: Work in pairs. One acts as Lin Qiang and the other acts as the passersby. Use the conversation structure shown below and the information in the table above to act out the conversation.

会话结构：

Conversation structure

行人一: 请问<u>中央公园</u>怎么走？

林强: <u>从这里直走</u>就到了。

行人一: 谢谢。

II. 情况：吴爱林和陈林正开车旅行。他们每天都会迷路。下方表格列出了他们每天想去的地点和他们跟谁问路。

Situation: Wu Ailin and Chen Lin are on a road trip. They get lost each day when they are on the way to a certain location. The table below shows the locations they want to go and who they ask for directions.

天数	他们想去的地点	他们跟谁问路
第一天	好好中国饭馆	行人
第二天	水族馆（aquarium）	饭馆收银员
第三天	美术馆	警察（police）
第四天	中国城（Chinatown）	司机（driver）
第五天	美美服装店	行人

任务：两人一组。一个人扮演吴爱林，另一个人扮演陈林。用上方的表格和下方的会话结构做角色扮演。

Task: Work in pairs. One acts as Wu Ailin and the other as Chen Lin. Use the information in the table above and the conversation structure listed below to act out the conversation.

会话结构：

Conversation structure:

吴爱林: 我们迷路了！

陈林: 我们停下来问<u>路人 好好中国饭馆</u>怎么走吧。

读写沟通活动 Literacy Communication Activities

I. 今天是王文乐第一天上课。他不确定教室在哪儿。他问了几个经过他身边的同学。帮王文乐在下方空格写下到教室的方向。

Today is Wang Wenle's first day of school. He is not sure where to go for different classes. He asks several students who pass by him. Help Wang Wenle write down the directions to the classes in the blanks below.

王文乐: 请问中文教室在哪儿?
学生: _____就到了。
　　　　(Go straight from here)

王文乐: 请问数学教室在哪儿?
学生: _____就到了。
　　　　(Take a left from here)

王文乐: 请问音乐教室在哪儿?
学生: _____就到了。
　　　　(Take a right first, and then go straight)

王文乐: 请问体育教室在哪儿?
学生: _____就到了。
　　　　(Take a left first, and then go straight)

II. 问你的老师怎么从学校的某个地点(例如:校长室、学生食堂、厕所走到教室。当你的老师回答你的问题时,把答案写在下面空格。写完后与你的同学们比较答案。你写对了吗?

Ask your teacher how to get to a certain location in school from your classroom (for example: principal's office, student cafeteria, bathroom). When your teacher answers your question, write down her answer in the space provided below. When you finish, compare your answers with your classmates. Did you get the direction correct?

你: _____怎么走?

你的老师: _____
_____

Lesson 4 I am Lost on the Road

讨论 Discussion

Xizhimen Bridge

It is easy to get lost in a big city. Many people would agree that the place one can easily get lost in Beijing, the capital city of China, is 西直门桥 (Xizhímén qiáo, Xizhimen Bridge). 西直门 (Xizhímén, Xizhimen) was a gate in the Beijing city wall and is now the name of the transportation node. The old 西直门桥 was built in the late 1970s. Due to the increasing traffic, the new 西直门桥 replaced the original bridge with the roundabout on top of it in 1999. However, because of the complex road designs of the bridge, drivers who are not familiar with the area can easily get lost for hours on the bridge.

Discussion Question:

1. What other big cities are there in China besides Beijing? Prepare a brief introduction of a city in China.

第五课 Lesson 5

春夏秋冬
Spring, Summer, Autumn and Winter

沟通任务 Communication Tasks

- Asking about one's favorite season.
- Stating what one can do in the seasons.
- Asking a certain item's available flavors in a store.
- Asking what one's favorite flavor of a certain food item is.
- Asking for the total of the items bought.
- Stating that some people have the same opinion as yours.

课前讨论 Warm-up Discussion Questions

1. What is your favorite season?
2. What do you like to do in your favorite season?
3. Do you like that people have the same opinions as yours?
4. Have you tasted moon cakes in Mid-Autumn Festival? What kind of flavors have you tried?

生词 Vocabulary

简体 (Simplified)	繁体 (Traditional)	拼音 (Pinyin)	释义 (Definition)	词性 (Parts of speech)	例句 (Examples)
1. 春天	春天	chūntiān	spring	n.	我喜欢春天。(I like spring.)
2. 夏天	夏天	xiàtiān	summer	n.	我不喜欢夏天。(I don't like summer.)
3. 秋天	秋天	qiūtiān	autumn	n.	秋天的景色很漂亮。(The scenery in the fall is very pretty.)
4. 冬天	冬天	dōngtiān	winter	n.	冬天很冷。(It is cold in winter.)
5. 最	最	zuì	the most	adv.	我最喜欢春天。(I like Spring most.)
6. 季节	季節	jìjié	season	n.	你最喜欢哪一个季节？(Which season is your favorite?)
7. 海边	海邊	hǎibiān	by the sea; at the beach; used to describe activities in or by the sea		夏天我可以去海边游泳。(I can go swimming in the sea in summer.)
8. 冲浪	冲浪	chōng làng	to surf		夏天我可以去海边冲浪。(I can go surfing in the sea in summer.)
9. 沙滩	沙灘	shātān	beach	n.	今天我去沙滩玩。(Today I went to play on the beach.)
10. 月饼	月餅	yuèbing	moon cake	n.	月饼很好吃。(Moon cakes are delicious.)
11. 赏月	賞月	shǎng yuè	to see and appreciate the Moon		我跟家人一起赏月。(I appreciate the Moon with my family.)
12. 花	花	huā	flower	n.	在春天我可以看到很多花。(I can see a lot of flowers in the spring.)
13. 蝴蝶	蝴蝶	húdié	butterfly	n.	在春天我可以看到很多蝴蝶。(I can see many butterflies in the spring.)

第五课 春夏秋冬
Lesson 5 Spring, Summer, Autumn and Winter

14. 元宵	元宵	yuánxiāo	glutinous rice ball	n.	我们在元宵节吃元宵。(We eat glutinous rice ball—Yuanxiao in Lantern Festival.)
15. 放	放	fàng	to set off	v.	在中国新年,我可以放鞭炮。(I can set off firecrackers at Chinese New Year.)
16. 舞龙舞狮	舞龍舞獅	wǔ lóng wǔ shī	dragon and lion dance		在中国新年,我可以看舞龙舞狮。(I can see the dragon and lion dance during Chinese New Year.)
17. 赏	賞	shǎng	to appreciate	v.	在元宵节,我可以吃元宵,也可以赏花灯。(I can eat glutinous rice balls and appreciate festive lanterns at the Lantern Festival.)
18. 气候	氣候	qìhòu	climate	n.	春天的气候不冷不热。(The spring climate is not cold or hot.)
19. 舒服	舒服	shūfu	comfortable	adj.	春天的气候很舒服。(The spring weather is comfortable.)
20. 口味	口味	kǒuwèi	flavor	n.	这家店的月饼有很多口味。(This store has many moon cake flavors.)
21. 传统	傳統	chuántǒng	traditional	adj.	传统口味的月饼有很多种。(There are many kinds of traditional-flavored moon cakes.)
22. 莲蓉	蓮蓉	liánróng	lotus seed	n.	莲蓉月饼很好吃。(Lotus seed flavored moon cakes are delicious.)
23. 豆沙	豆沙	dòushā	red bean	n.	我喜欢吃豆沙月饼。(I like to eat red bean moon cakes.)
24. 枣泥	棗泥	zǎoní	jujube	n.	我爸爸喜欢吃枣泥月饼。(My father likes to eat jujube moon cakes.)
25. 冰淇淋	冰淇淋	bīngqílín	ice cream	n.	我妈妈喜欢吃冰淇淋月饼。(My mother likes to eat ice cream moon cakes.)
26. 盒	盒	hé	box	m.w.	我买了一盒月饼。(I bought a box of moon cakes.)

27. 总共	總共	zǒnggòng	in total	*adv.*	两盒月饼总共多少钱？(How much is the total for two boxes of moon cakes?)
29. 有的	有的	yǒude	some	*pron.*	有的人喜欢吃月饼,有的人不喜欢吃月饼。(Some people like to eat moon cakes, and some don't.)
30. 跟……一样……	跟……一樣……	gēn... yíyàng...	same as ...		有的人跟我一样喜欢春天。(Some people like spring just as I do.)
31. 美丽	美麗	měilì	beautiful	*adj.*	我觉得春天很美丽！(I feel spring is very beautiful!)

专有名词 Proper Nouns

简体 (Simplified)	繁体 (Traditional)	拼音 (Pinyin)	释义 (Definition)	词性 (Parts of speech)	例句 (Examples)
1. 中秋节	中秋節	Zhōngqiū Jié	Mid-Autumn Festival	*p.n.*	秋天我可以庆祝中秋节。(I can celebrate Mid-Autumn Festival in the fall.)
2. 元宵节	元宵節	Yuánxiāo Jié	Lantern Festival	*p.n.*	冬天我可以庆祝元宵节。(I can celebrate the Lantern Festival in the winter.)

补充词语 Supplementary Vocabulary

Simplified	Traditional	Pinyin	Definition
1. 草莓	草莓	cǎoméi	strawberry (*n.*)
2. 香草	香草	xiāngcǎo	vanilla (*n.*)
3. 水蜜桃	水蜜桃	shuǐmìtáo	peach (*n.*)
4. 柠檬	檸檬	níngméng	lemon (*n.*)
5. 葡萄	葡萄	pútao	grape (*n.*)
6. 樱桃	櫻桃	yīngtao	cherry (*n.*)

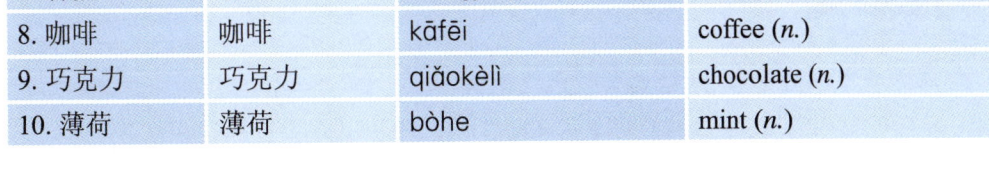

7. 香蕉	香蕉	xiāngjiāo	banana (*n.*)
8. 咖啡	咖啡	kāfēi	coffee (*n.*)
9. 巧克力	巧克力	qiǎokèlì	chocolate (*n.*)
10. 薄荷	薄荷	bòhe	mint (*n.*)

沟通任务 Communication Tasks

I Asking about one's favorite season

Question: 春、夏、秋、冬你最喜欢哪一个季节？

(Which season do you like most: Spring, summer, autumn or winter?)

Answer: 我最喜欢_____。

(I like _____ most.)

Example:

Question: 春、夏、秋、冬你最喜欢哪一个季节？

(Which season do you like most: Spring, summer, autumn or winter?)

Answer: 我最喜欢<u>夏天</u>。

(I like <u>Summer</u> most.)

Practice: Ask a friend in class which season is their favorite.

II Stating what one can do in the seasons

夏天我可以去_____。

(I can _____ in the summer.)

秋天我可以_____。

(I can _____ in the fall.)

春天我可以_____。

(I can _____ in the spring.)

冬天我可以_____。

(I can _____ in the winter.)

> **Examples:**

夏天我可以去海边冲浪,也可以在沙滩玩沙。

(I can go surfing in the sea and play in the sand on the beach in the summer.)

春天我可以看到很多花和蝴蝶。

(I can see a lot of flowers and butterflies in the spring.)

Elaborated answers:

秋天我可以庆祝中秋节。我可以跟家人一起吃月饼和赏月。

(I can celebrate Mid-autumn Festival in the fall. I can eat moon cakes and see the moon with my family.)

冬天我可以庆祝中国新年和元宵节。在中国新年我可以放鞭炮,也可以看舞龙舞狮。在元宵节我可以吃元宵,也可以赏花灯。

(I can celebrate Chinese New Year and the Lantern Festival in the winter. I can set off firecrackers and see the dragon and lion dance at Chinese New Year. I can eat glutinous rice balls and appreciate festive lanterns at the Lantern Festival.)

Practice: Use the sentence structure above to describe what you do in your favorite season.

III Asking a certain item's available flavors in a store

这家店的_____有什么口味?

(What _____ flavors does this store have?)

我们有_____。

(We have _____ flavors.)

> **Examples:**

这家店的月饼有什么口味?

(What moon cake flavors does this store have?)

我们有传统口味也有新口味。

(We have the traditional and the new flavors.)

Elaborated answer:

我们有传统口味也有新口味。传统口味的月饼有莲蓉月饼、豆沙月饼和枣泥月饼。新口味的月饼有绿茶月饼和冰淇淋月饼。

(We have the traditional and the new flavors. The traditional moon cake flavors include the lotus seed, red bean, and jujube moon cakes . The new moon cake flavors include green tea and ice cream moon cakes.)

Practice: The moon cake store you and your friends will talk about has the ice cream

Lesson 5 Spring, Summer, Autumn and Winter
第五课 春夏秋冬

and the jujube moon cakes. Have a conversation about the moon cake flavors using the structure introduced above.

IV) Asking what one's favorite flavor of a certain food item is

Question: 你最爱吃哪一种_____?

(What kind of _____ do you love to eat most?)

Answer: 我最爱吃_____。

(I love to eat _____ most.)

Example:

Question: 你最爱吃哪一种<u>月饼</u>?

(Which kind of <u>moon cake</u> do you love to eat most?)

Answer: 我最爱吃<u>冰淇淋</u>月饼。

(I love to eat <u>ice cream</u> moon cake most.)

Practice: Ask a friend in class which kind of moon cake is his or her favorite.

V) Asking for the total of the items bought

Question: 我要买_____。总共多少钱?

(I want to buy _____. How much is the total?)

Answer: 总共_____元。

(The total is _____ dollars.)

Example:

Question: 我要买<u>两盒冰淇淋月饼</u>。总共多少钱?

(I want to buy <u>two boxes of ice cream moon cakes</u>. How much is the total?)

Answer: 总共<u>200</u>元。

(The total is <u>200</u> dollars.)

Practice: A box of red bean moon cakes is 50 dollars. Tell the classmate next to you that you want to buy two boxes and ask how much it is.

VI) Stating that some people have the same opinion as yours

有的人跟我一样_____。

(Some people _____ just as I do.)

Examples:

有的人跟我一样<u>喜欢春天</u>。

65

(Some people <u>like spring</u> just as I do.)

有的人跟我一样<u>不喜欢春天</u>。

(Some people <u>don't like spring</u> just as I do.)

Practice: Translate the following sentence into Chinese, "Some people like winter just as I do."

情景(一) Scenario 1

王老师正和他的学生们讨论他们最喜欢的季节。

王老师：春、夏、秋、冬你们最喜欢哪一个季节？

李小明：我最喜欢夏天，因为夏天我可以去海边冲浪，也可以在沙滩玩沙。

张爱华：我最喜欢秋天，因为秋天我可以庆祝中秋节。我可以跟家人一起吃月饼和赏月。

王文丽：我最喜欢春天，因为春天我可以看到很多花和蝴蝶。

吴家玲：我最喜欢冬天，因为冬天我可以庆祝中国新年和元宵节。在中国新年我可以放鞭炮，也可以看舞龙舞狮。在元宵节我可以吃元宵，也可以赏花灯。

李小明：王老师，春、夏、秋、冬，你最喜欢哪一个季节？

王老师：我最喜欢春天。因为春天的气候不冷不热，最舒服。

Comprehension Questions

1. 为什么张爱华喜欢秋天？
2. 王老师喜欢哪一个季节？

情景(二) Scenario 2

张爱华和他妈妈正准备庆祝中秋节。他们在饼店里买月饼。

妈　妈：请问这家店的月饼有什么口味？

店　员：我们有传统口味也有新口味。传统口味的月饼有莲蓉月饼、豆沙月饼和枣泥月饼。新口味的月饼有绿茶月饼和冰淇淋月饼。

妈　妈：爱华，你最爱吃哪一种月饼？

张爱华：我最爱吃冰淇淋月饼。

妈　妈：我们要买两盒冰淇淋月饼。请问多少钱？

店　员：总共两百元。

Comprehension Questions

1. 店里的月饼有什么口味？
2. 妈妈买了哪一种月饼？

第五课 春夏秋冬
Lesson 5 Spring, Summer, Autumn and Winter

情景（三）Scenario 3

王老师正在写他的日记……

王老师的日记

  今天我问了学生们他们最喜欢哪一个季节。有的人喜欢冬天，有的人喜欢夏天，有的人喜欢秋天，有的人跟我一样喜欢春天。我觉得春天最美丽！

王老师

Comprehension Questions

1. 今天王老师问了学生们什么问题？
2. 王老师觉得哪一个季节最美丽？

口语沟通活动 Oral Communication Activities

I. 情况：你想知道你的同学们最喜欢哪个季节。

Situation: You want to learn about your classmates' favorite seasons.

任务：在教室问几个同学，"春、夏、秋、冬，你最喜欢哪一个季节？"。在下方表格写下他们的名字并勾选他们最喜欢的季节。

Task: Walk around the classroom to survey your classmates about their favorite seasons by asking, "春、夏、秋、冬，你最喜欢哪一个季节？". Write down their names in the table below and put a check mark under the answer they provide.

姓名	春	夏	秋	冬
1.				
2.				
3.				
4.				
5.				
6.				
7.				
8.				

9.				
10.				

各有几个人说春、夏、秋和冬是他们最喜欢的季节？在下方表格写出人数并用下列句型结构在课堂上做报告："__个人最喜欢春天"，"__个人最喜欢夏天"，"__个人最喜欢秋天"，"__个人最喜欢冬天"。

How many people you surveyed answered 春, 夏, 秋 and 冬 as their favorite season? Write down the numbers in the table below and report your findings to the class using the sentence structure, "__个人最喜欢春天"，"__个人最喜欢夏天"，"__个人最喜欢秋天"，"__个人最喜欢冬天".

	春	夏	秋	冬
人数 __of people				

II. 情况：吴爱林是冰淇淋店的店员。这家店有十种冰淇淋口味（请参考下方表格）。

Situation: Wu Ailin is working in an ice cream store. The ice cream store has 10 ice cream flavors (see the flavors listed below).

冰淇淋口味	
草莓（strawberry）	樱桃（cherry）
香草（vanilla）	香蕉（banana）
水蜜桃（peach）	咖啡（coffee）
柠檬（lemon）	巧克力（chocolate）
葡萄（grape）	薄荷（mint）

今天五位客人来店里买他们最喜欢的冰淇淋。把他们最爱的口味、买几盒和消费总额列在下表。

Five customers came to the store to buy their favorite ice cream flavors today. Their favorite ice cream flavors, the number of boxes of ice cream they bought, and the total prices are in the table below.

客人	最喜欢的口味	盒数	消费总额
客人一	香草	三盒	150元

第五课 春夏秋冬
Lesson 5 Spring, Summer, Autumn and Winter

客人二	葡萄	一盒	100元
客人三	咖啡	两盒	100元
客人四	樱桃	一盒	50元
客人五	薄荷	五盒	250元

任务：两人一组。一个人扮演吴爱林，另一个人扮演客人。用上方表格的资讯和下方列出的会话结构做角色扮演。

Task: Work in pairs. One acts as Wu Ailin and the other as customers. Use the information in the table above and the conversation structure listed below to act out the conversation.

会话结构：

Conversation structure:

客人一：这家店的冰淇淋有什么口味？

吴爱林：我们有草莓、香草、水蜜桃、柠檬、葡萄、樱桃、香蕉、咖啡、巧克力、和薄荷口味。你最爱吃哪一种冰淇淋？

客人一：我最爱吃香草冰淇淋。我要买三盒香草冰淇淋。总共多少钱？

吴爱林：总共150元。

读写沟通活动 Literacy Communication Activities

I. 王文乐今天的中文作业是与同学讨论彼此喜欢和不喜欢什么，并写一书面报告。王文乐发觉班上一些同学跟他的想法一样。帮助王文乐在下面完成他的报告。

Wang Wenle's Chinese homework today is to discuss his likes and dislikes with his classmates, and write a report on whether people in class have the same opinions. Wang Wenle found that some of his classmates have the same opinions as he does. Help Wang Wenle write his report in Chinese in the blanks provided below.

王文乐的报告

1. 有的人跟我一样＿＿＿＿＿＿＿＿＿＿＿＿＿＿。

    (like winter)

2. 有的人跟我一样＿＿＿＿＿＿＿＿＿＿＿＿＿＿。

    (don't like skiing)

3. 有的人跟我一样＿＿＿＿＿＿＿＿＿＿＿＿＿＿。

    (like eating moon cakes)

4. 有的人跟我一样_____。
　　　　　　　　　　(don't like summer)
5. 有的人跟我一样_____。
　　　　　　　　　　(like studying Chinese)

II. 春、夏、秋、冬，你最喜欢哪一个季节？请在下面回答并画出你最喜欢的季节和你在这个季节做些什么活动。

Answer the question using the sentence structure provided below, and draw your favorite season and what you can do in the season in the space below.

我最喜欢_____，因为我可以_____

_____

_____

_____

Lesson 5 Spring, Summer, Autumn and Winter

Discussion

The Chinese Moon Festival

The Chinese Moon Festival, also called the Mid-Autumn Festival, is on the 15th of the 8th lunar month when the moon is at its fullest and roundest. The Chinese Moon Festival celebration is associated with the legend of Houyi and Chang'e. Legend says that a long time ago, a hero named Houyi shot down nine of ten Suns in the sky saving people who were dying from heat. In order to thank Houyi, the queen of heaven gave him a bottle of elixir which could make him immortal. Houyi asked his wife, Chang'e, to keep the elixir in a safe place. However, one day one of Houyi's students, Feng Meng, tried to force Chang'e to give him the elixir while Houyi had gone hunting. Chang'e did not want to give Feng Meng the elixir so she drank it immediately. Later Chang'e became an immortal and flew to the Moon. From then on, people often pray to the Moon and Chang'e for fortune and safety. During the Mid-Autumn Festival, Chinese family members and friends will gather to admire the bright Moon, eat moon cakes, and try to see if they can see Chang'e on the moon.

Discussion Question:

1. There are several versions of the legend of Houyi and Chang'e. Ask any Chinese native speakers you know about the legend or search for the legend online. How many versions of the legend are there? Compare the different versions you heard with the ones your classmates heard.

第六课
Lesson 6

你妈妈要你买什么?
What Did Your Mom Ask You to Buy?

沟通任务 Communication Tasks

- Asking what things someone wants you to buy.
- Asking what one wants to buy in a certain store.
- Asking for help and stating what you are going to do.
- Asking if a certain item is available.
- Asking when something will be restocked.
- Stating things you will do in order.

课前讨论 Warm-up Discussion Questions

1. Have you helped your parents shop for groceries? Did you find the items you needed in the supermarket?
2. What do you do if the items you need to buy are out of stock?

第六课 你妈妈要你买什么?
Lesson 6 What Did Your Mom Ask You to Buy?

生词 Vocabulary

简体 (Simplified)	繁体 (Traditional)	拼音 (Pinyin)	释义 (Definition)	词性 (Parts of speech)	例句 (Examples)
1. 购物	購物	gòu wù	to shop		你要去哪儿购物? (Where do you go shopping?)
2. 清单	清單	qīngdān	list	n.	我看一下我的购物清单。(Let me take a look at my shopping list.)
3. 条	條	tiáo	classifier for fish	m.w.	我得买一条鱼。(I have to buy a fish.)
4. 鱼	魚	yú	fish	n.	我有三条鱼。(I have three fish.)
5. 把	把	bǎ	classifier for anything that can be held in one's hand	m.w.	我得买一把葱。(I have to buy a handful of spring onions.)
6. 葱	蔥	cōng	spring onion	n.	我有两把葱。(I have two handfuls of spring onions.)
7. 根	根	gēn	classifier for long objects	m.w.	这根胡萝卜很大。(This carrot is big.)
8. 胡萝卜	胡蘿蔔	húluóbo	carrot	n.	你有几根胡萝卜? (How many carrots do you have?)
9. 颗	顆	kē	classifier for small spheres	m.w.	请给我一颗洋葱。(Please give me an onion.)
10. 洋葱	洋蔥	yángcōng	onion	n.	我得买一颗洋葱。(I have to buy an onion.)
11. 瓶	瓶	píng	bottle	n.	请给我一瓶可乐。(Please give me a bottle of coke.)
12. 米酒	米酒	mǐjiǔ	rice wine	n.	我得买一瓶米酒。(I have to buy a bottle of rice wine.)
13. 蕃茄酱	蕃茄醬	fānqiéjiàng	ketchup	n.	我有三瓶蕃茄酱。(I have three bottles of ketchup.)
14. 土豆	土豆	tǔdòu	potato	n.	我得买三个土豆。(I have to buy three potatoes.)
15. 斤	斤	jīn	pound	m.w.	我爸爸买了一斤火腿。(My father bought a pound of ham.)

73

16. 火腿	火腿	huǒtuǐ	ham	n.	我爸爸给了我一斤火腿。(My father gave me a pound of ham.)
18. 袋	袋	dài	bag	n.	我弟弟买了一袋米。(My younger brother bough a bag of rice.)
19. 米	米	mǐ	rice	n.	我弟弟给了我一袋米。(My younger brother gave me a bag of rice.)
20. 柳橙汁	柳橙汁	liǔchéngzhī	orange juice	n.	我朋友买了三瓶柳橙汁。(My friend bought three bottles of orange juice.)
21. 重	重	zhòng	heavy	adj.	米很重。(Rice is heavy.)
22. 辆	輛	liàng	classifier for carts	m.w.	我们去找一辆购物车吧。(Let's look for a shopping cart.)
23. 购物车	購物車	gòuwùchē	shopping cart	n.	这辆购物车很大。(This shopping cart is big.)
25. 烤肉	烤肉	kǎo ròu	to barbeque		我们要烤肉庆祝我爸爸的生日。(We want to have a barbeque to celebrate my father's birthday.)
26. 蛋糕	蛋糕	dàngāo	cake	n.	我要买一个巧克力蛋糕。(I want to buy a chocolate cake.)
27. 推	推	tuī	to push	v.	请你帮我推一辆购物车。(Please help me push the shopping cart.)
28. 生鲜区	生鮮區	shēngxiān qū	raw food section	n.	我先到生鲜区买牛肉。(I am going to the raw food section to buy beef first.)
29. 全	全	quán	all	adv.	牛肉今天全都卖完了。(All the beef has been sold today.)
30. 进货	進貨	jìn huò	to restock		牛肉什么时候会进货？(When will the beef be restocked?)
31. 可能	可能	kěnéng	possibly	adv.	牛肉可能明天早上会进货。(The beef will be restocked possibly tomorrow morning.)

第六课 你妈妈要你买什么?
Lesson 6 What Did Your Mom Ask You to Buy?

专有名词 Proper Nouns

简体 (Simplified)	繁体 (Traditional)	拼音 (Pinyin)	释义 (Definition)	词性 (Parts of speech)	例句 (Examples)
1. 沃尔玛	沃爾瑪	Wò'ērmǎ	Wal-Mart	p.n.	我们现在去沃尔玛吧。(Let's go to Wal-Mart now.)

补充词语 Supplementary Vocabulary

Simplified	Traditional	Pinyin	Definition
1. 葡萄汁	葡萄汁	pútaozhī	grape juice (n.)
2. 酱油	醬油	jiàngyóu	soy sauce (n.)
3. 醋	醋	cù	vinegar (n.)
4. 青菜	青菜	qīngcài	leafy green (n.)
5. 饼干	餅乾	bǐnggān	cookie; cracker (n.)
6. 包	包	bāo	bag (m.w.)
7. 方便面	方便麵	fāngbiànmiàn	instant noodle (n.)
8. 苹果	蘋果	píngguǒ	apple (n.)
9. 豆腐	豆腐	dòufu	tofu (n.)
10. 豆干	豆干	dòugān	dried tofu (n.)
11. 糖果	糖果	tángguǒ	candy (n.)
12. 柠檬	檸檬	níngméng	lemon (n.)
13. 西瓜	西瓜	xīguā	watermelon (n.)
14. 冷冻比萨饼	冷凍比薩餅	lěngdòng bǐsàbǐng	frozen pizza (n.)
15. 冰	冰	bīng	ice (n.)
16. 香肠	香腸	xiāngcháng	sausage (n.)
17. 罐	罐	guàn	jar (m.w.)
18. 盐	鹽	yán	salt (n.)

沟通任务 Communication Tasks

I) Asking what things someone wants you to buy

Question: _____要你买什么？
(What did _____ ask you to buy?)
Answer: _____要我买_____。
(_____ asked me to buy _____.)

Example:

Question: 你妈妈要你买什么？
(What did your mom ask you to buy?)

Answer 1: 我妈妈要我买两个土豆、一斤火腿、一盒蛋、一袋米和三瓶柳橙汁。
(My mom asked me to buy two potatoes, a pound of ham, a box of eggs, a bag of rice and three bottles of orange juice.)

Answer 2: 我妈妈要我买一条鱼、一把葱、四根胡萝卜、两颗洋葱、一瓶米酒和一瓶蕃茄酱。
(My mom asked me to buy a fish, a handful of spring onions, four carrots, two onions, a bottle of rice wine and a bottle of ketchup.)

Practice: Work in pairs. Ask each other what your mom asked you to buy and pick a food item to answer your partner.

II) Asking what one wants to buy in a certain store

Question: _____要去_____买什么？
(What is/are _____ going to buy in _____?)
Answer: _____要去_____买_____。
(_____ want(s) to go to _____ buy _____.)

Example:

Question: 我们要去沃尔玛买什么？
(What are we going to buy in Wal-Mart?)
Answer: 我们要去沃尔玛买一些牛肉。
(We want to go to Wal-Mart to buy some beef.)

Elaborated Answer:
我们要买一些牛肉,因为明天是你爷爷的生日。我们要烤肉庆祝他的生日。我

第六课 你妈妈要你买什么?
Lesson 6 What Did Your Mom Ask You to Buy?

们还要买一个巧克力生日蛋糕,因为你爷爷最喜欢巧克力口味。
(We want to buy some beef because tomorrow is your grandfather's birthday. We want to have a barbeque to celebrate his birthday. We also want to buy a chocolate cake because chocolate is your grandfather's favorite flavor.)

Practice: Work in pairs. Ask each other what you are going to buy in a grocery store you usually go to.

III Asking for help and stating what you are going to do

请你帮我_____。我先到_____。
(Please help me _____. I am going to _____ first.)

Example:

请你帮我推一辆购物车。我先到生鲜区买牛肉。
(Please help me push the cart. I am going to buy beef in the raw food section first.)

Practice: Work in pairs. Translate the following sentence into Chinese, "Please help me push the cart. I am going to buy some pork in the raw food section". Ask your teacher if your translation is correct.

IV Asking if a certain item is available

Question: 请问还有_____吗?
 (Is there still _____?)
Positive Answer: 还有。
 (Yes, there is.)
Negative Answer:对不起,_____今天全都卖完了。
 (Sorry, _____ is sold out today.)

Example:

Question: 请问还有牛肉吗?
 (Is there still beef?)
Positive Answer: 还有。
 (Yes, there is.)
Negative Answer:对不起,牛肉今天全都卖完了。
 (Sorry, the beef is sold out today.)

Practice: Ask the classmate sitting next to you if there are still beef burgers. The answer could be either positive or negative.

V Asking when something will be restocked

Question：什么时候会进货？
　　　　　(When will it be restocked?)
Answer：可能_____以后。
　　　　　(Possibly after _____.)

Example:

Question：什么时候会进货？
　　　　　(When will it be restocked?)
Answer：可能明天早上十点以后。
　　　　　(Possibly after 10 am tomorrow.)

Practice: Ask a classmate, "When will it be restocked?", and your classmate will answer, "Possibly after 7 am tomorrow".

VI Stating things you will do in order

_____我先_____，_____我_____。
(_____ I bought the chocolate birthday cake first, and then _____, I will_____.)

Example:

今天我先买了巧克力生日蛋糕，明天早上我再去沃尔玛买牛肉。
(Today I bought the chocolate birthday cake first, and then tomorrow morning, I will go to Wal-Mart to buy beef.)

Practice: Work in pairs and take turns to read aloud the sentence in the example above.

情景（一）Scenario 1

李小明和张爱华要买妈妈给他们的购物清单上的东西。

李小明：爱华，你妈妈要你买什么？

张爱华：我看一下我的购物清单……我妈妈要我买一条鱼、一把葱、四根胡萝卜、两颗洋葱、一瓶米酒和一瓶蕃茄酱。你呢？

张爱华：我妈妈要我买两个土豆、一斤火腿、一盒蛋、一袋米和三瓶柳橙汁。

李小明：米很重，我们去找一辆购物车吧。

第六课 你妈妈要你买什么?
Lesson 6　What Did Your Mom Ask You to Buy?

Comprehension Questions

1. 张爱华的购物清单有什么?
2. 李小明的妈妈要李小明买什么?

情景(二) Scenario 2

吴家玲和她妈妈正要去沃尔玛买东西。

吴家玲： 妈妈,今天我们要去沃尔玛买什么?

妈　妈： 我们要买一些牛肉,因为明天是你爷爷的生日,我们要烤肉庆祝他的生日。
我们还要买一个巧克力生日蛋糕,因为你爷爷最喜欢巧克力口味。

他们到了沃尔玛……

妈　妈： 家玲,请你帮我推一辆购物车。我先到生鲜区买牛肉。

吴家玲： 好。

吴家玲的妈妈在生鲜区……

妈　妈： 请问还有牛肉吗?

店　员： 对不起,牛肉今天全都卖完了。

妈　妈： 什么时候会进货?

店　员： 可能明天早上十点以后。

Comprehension Questions

1. 明天是谁的生日?
2. 妈妈要买什么?
3. 牛肉什么时候会进货?

情景(三) Scenario 3

吴家玲的妈妈正在写她的日记……

妈妈的日记

明天是吴家玲爷爷的烤肉生日会。今天我想在沃尔玛买牛肉和巧克力生日蛋糕,但是沃尔玛的牛肉全都卖完了。所以今天我先买了巧克力生日蛋糕,明天早上我再去沃尔玛买牛肉。

Comprehension Questions

1. 妈妈买了什么口味的蛋糕?
2. 明天早上妈妈要去沃尔玛买什么?

口语沟通活动 Oral Communication Activities

I. 情况:一群朋友们要帮他们的家人买菜。下表列出了家人请他们帮忙买的东西。

Situation: A group of friends are going to help their family members buy groceries. The table below shows which of their family members ask for help and what things they need.

姓名	家人	东西
陈林	妈妈	一瓶葡萄汁(grape juice) 一瓶酱油(soy sauce) 一瓶醋(vinegar) 两斤猪肉 一把青菜(leafy green)
林丽	爸爸	一盒饼干 三包(bag)方便面 五颗苹果(apple) 一盒豆腐 一包豆干(dried tofu)
张爱友	姐姐	一包糖果(candy) 三颗柠檬(lemon) 一颗西瓜(watermelon) 一个冷冻比萨饼(frozen pizza) 一盒冰淇淋
沈心宜	外婆	两盒绿茶月饼 一包冰(ice) 十条香肠(sausage) 一袋米 一罐(jar)盐(salt)

任务:四人一组。每个人挑一个角色来扮演。用表格里的内容和下方的会话结构来做角色扮演。

Lesson 6 What Did Your Mom Ask You to Buy?
第六课 你妈妈要你买什么？

Task: Work in groups of 4. Each person picks one of the roles listed in the table above. Use the information in the table and the conversation structure below to act out the conversation.

会话结构：

Conversation structure:

陈林：<u>你爸爸要你买什么？</u>
林丽：<u>我爸爸要我买一盒饼干、三包方便面、五个苹果、一盒豆腐和一包豆干。</u>
林丽：<u>你妈妈要你买什么？</u>
陈林：<u>我妈妈要我买一瓶葡萄汁、一瓶酱油、一瓶醋、两斤猪肉和一把青菜。</u>

II. 情况：吴爱林正在买东西，但是她找不到她想买的东西。她想问店员这些东西店里有没有。

Situation: Wu Ailin is doing her grocery shopping and can't find several items she needs to buy. She wants to ask the staff in the supermarket if the items are available.

任务：两人一组。一个人扮演吴爱林，另一个人扮演店员。下表列出了吴爱林要买的东西，这些东西是否卖完了，还有这些东西什么时候进的货。用下表的信息和列出的会话结构作角色扮演。

Task: Work in pairs. One acts as Wu Ailin and the other as the staff. The table below shows the items Wu Ailin needs to buy, whether or not the items are in stock, and when they will be restocked. Use the information in the table and the conversation structure listed below to act out the conversation.

东西	还有没有？	进货时间
鸡肉	卖完了	明天下午三点以后
苹果	卖完了	明天早上九点以后
冰淇淋	还有	
方便面	卖完了	今天晚上七点以后
酱油	卖完了	后天早上八点以后
猪肉	卖完了	后天早上十点以后

会话结构:

Conversation structure:

吴爱林: 请问还有鸡肉吗?
店员: 对不起,鸡肉今天全都卖完了。
吴爱林: 什么时候会进货?
店员: 可能明天下午三点以后。

读写沟通活动 Literacy Communication Activities

I. 王文乐在沃尔玛买了一些他要的东西,但是有些东西他得明天去买。王文乐写了小字条提醒自己什么东西已经买了,什么还没买,但是一些汉字他忘了怎么写。请帮王文乐完成下面的小字条。

Wang Wenle has bought some of the food items he needs in Wal-Mart, but still has some he needs to buy tomorrow. Wang Wenle wants to write down notes in Chinese to remind himself about what he has bought and what he still needs to buy, but Wang Wenle forgot how to write some of the characters. Help Wang Wenle complete the notes below.

今天　　　　　　　　　　明天上午

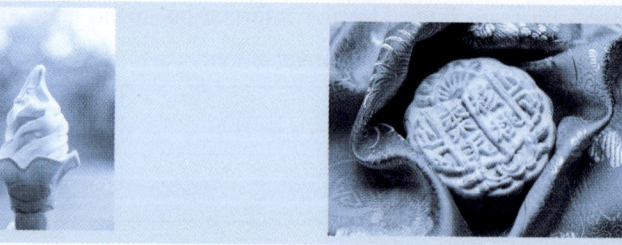

今天我先买了_____,_____我再去沃尔玛买_____。

昨天　　　　　　　　　　明天下午

今天我先买了_____,_____我再去沃尔玛买_____。

Lesson 6 第六课 你妈妈要你买什么?
What Did Your Mom Ask You to Buy?

今天　　　　　　　　　　　　　　明天晚上

今天我先买了_____，_____我再去沃尔玛买_____。

昨天　　　　　　　　　　　　　　明天中午

今天我先买了_____，_____我再去沃尔玛买_____。

II. 如果你想请一个朋友帮你买东西,你会请他帮你买什么？ 在下面列出你需要的东西。

If you had the opportunity to ask a friend to grocery shop for you, what would you ask him or her to buy? Make your grocery list in the empty box below.

例子：

我要买……

1. 一盒蛋
2. 两斤牛肉

我要买...

1. _____
2. _____
3. _____

4. _____
5. _____
6. _____
7. _____
8. _____
9. _____
10. _____

讨论 Discussion

Wet Market in China

In China, many local residents visit their local wet market instead of supermarket each day to buy fresh meats and produce. Each city has several of these wet markets that service a range of neighborhoods. Many of the traditional markets not only sell food products, but also items such as kitchen appliances, flowers, and clothes.

Several things are unique to wet markets. First, the foods in a traditional market can be laid on a cloth on the ground or on concrete tables. The prices are usually not labeled. Customers choose what they want and the vendors weigh the item in front of the customers to tell them the price. Second, meat is fresh and not refrigerated. Sometimes customers can pick which livestock they want to purchase.

Discussion Question:

1. Turn the classroom into a Chinese market. Part of the class act as vendors and the rest act as customers. Decide as a class what food products the vendors will sell. The communication between vendors and customers should be in Chinese.

动物园

沟通任务 Communication Tasks

- Stating what you forgot to mention to someone.
- Asking someone to show their ID.
- Asking what areas or exhibition halls the zoo has.
- Stating what animals are in which areas or exhibition halls.
- Asking which of the places in the zoo is closest to your current location.
- Stating what animals one saw in certain places in the zoo.
- Stating that things one saw, happened when the person was in a certain place.
- Describing how something or someone is.

课前讨论 Warm-up Discussion Questions

1. Do you like visiting the zoo to see animals?
2. What areas or exhibition halls in the zoo do you like to visit most? What animals do you like to see?

第七课 动物园
Lesson 7 The Zoo

生词 Vocabulary

简体 (Simplified)	繁体 (Traditional)	拼音 (Pinyin)	释义 (Definition)	词性 (Parts of speech)	例句 (Examples)
1. 门票	門票	ménpiào	ticket	n.	我们要买两张门票。(We want to buy two tickets.)
2. 学生票	學生票	xuéshēng piào	student ticket	n.	我们买了两张学生票。(We bought two student tickets.)
3. 检票口	檢票口	jiǎnpiàokǒu	ticket checking entrance	n.	检票口在这儿。(The ticket checking entrance is here.)
4. 进去	進去	jìnqù	to enter	v.	我们进去吧。(Let's enter.)
5. 出示	出示	chūshì	to show	v.	请出示你们的门票。(Please show your tickets.)
6. 学生证	學生證	xuéshēng zhèng	student ID	n.	请出示你们的学生证。(Please show your student ID.)
7. 动物园	動物園	dòngwù yuán	zoo	n.	我想去动物园。(I want to go to the zoo.)
8. 哪些	哪些	nǎxiē	which	pron.	你想看哪些动物？(Which animals do you want to see?)
9. 区	區	qū	area	n.	这一区有哪些动物？(Which animals are in this area?)
10. 游客服务中心	遊客服務中心	yóukè fúwù zhōngxīn	tourist information center		我们去游客服务中心。(Let's go to the tourist information center.)
11. 馆	舘	guǎn	exhibition hall	n.	请问这家动物园有哪些馆？(What exhibition halls are there in this zoo?)
12. 大熊猫	大熊貓	dàxióngmāo	giant panda	n.	这家动物园有大熊猫馆。(This zoo has an giant panda exhibition hall.)
13. 企鹅	企鵝	qǐ'é	penguin	n.	这家动物园有企鹅馆。(This zoo has a penguin exhibition hall.)

87

14. 海洋	海洋	hǎiyáng	sea	n.	这家动物园有海洋馆。(This zoo has a sea exhibition hall.)
15. 鸟类	鳥類	niǎolèi	birds	n.	这家动物园有鸟类馆。(This zoo has a birds exhibition hall.)
16. 长颈鹿	長頸鹿	chángjǐnglù	giraffe	n.	我喜欢长颈鹿。(I like giraffes.)
17. 斑马	斑馬	bānmǎ	zebra	n.	我妹妹喜欢斑马。(My younger sister likes zebras.)
18. 鸵鸟	鴕鳥	tuóniǎo	ostrich	n.	我弟弟喜欢鸵鸟。(My younger brother likes ostriches.)
19. 无尾熊	無尾熊	wúwěixióng	koala	n.	我们都喜欢无尾熊。(We all like koalas.)
20. 海豚	海豚	hǎitún	dolphin	n.	海豚在海洋馆。(Dolphins are in the sea exhibition hall.)
21. 棕熊	棕熊	zōngxióng	brown bear	n.	棕熊在美洲动物区。(Brown bears are in the American animals area.)
22. 白老虎	白老虎	bái lǎohǔ	white tiger	n.	白老虎在亚洲动物区。(White tigers are in the Asian animals area.)
23. 红鹤	紅鶴	hónghè	flamingo	n.	红鹤在鸟类馆。(Flamingos are in the birds exhibition hall.)
24. 地方	地方	dìfang	place	n.	你想先去哪个地方？(Which place do you want to go first?)
25. 离	離	lí	from	prep.	哪个地方离我们最远？(Which place is furthest from us?)
26. 近	近	jìn	close	adj.	哪个地方离我们最近？(Which place is closest to us?)
27. 查	查	chá	to check	v.	我们查一查字典吧。(Let's check the dictionary.)
28. 地图	地圖	dìtú	map	n.	我们查一查地图吧。(Let's check the map.)
29. 只	隻	zhī	classifier for animals	m.w.	这家动物园有三只无尾熊。(This zoo has three koalas.)

第七课 动物园
Lesson 7 The Zoo

简体	繁体	拼音	释义	词性	例句
30. 正在	正在	zhèngzài	in the process of	prep.	这两只老虎正在玩。(These two tigers are playing.)
31. 竹子	竹子	zhúzi	bamboo	n.	两只熊猫正在竹子旁边玩。(Two pandas are playing next to the bamboo.)
32. 旁边	旁邊	pángbiān	near by position	n.	他正在电视旁边看书。(He is reading a book next to the TV.)
33. 玩耍	玩耍	wánshuǎ	to play	v.	熊猫喜欢一起玩耍。(Pandas like to play together.)
34. 可爱	可愛	kě'ài	cute	adj.	什么动物最可爱？(What animal is the cutest?)

专有名词 Proper Nouns

简体 (Simplified)	繁体 (Traditional)	拼音 (Pinyin)	释义 (Definition)	词性 (Parts of speech)	例句 (Examples)
1. 非洲	非洲	Fēizhōu	Africa	p.n.	这家动物园有非洲动物区。(This zoo has an African animals area.)
2. 美洲	美洲	Měizhōu	America	p.n.	这家动物园有美洲动物区。(This zoo has an American animals area.)
3. 澳洲	澳洲	Àozhōu	Australia	p.n.	这家动物园有澳洲动物区。(This zoo has an Australian animals area.)
4. 亚洲	亞洲	Yàzhōu	Asia	p.n.	这家动物园有亚洲动物区。(This zoo has an Asian animals area.)
5. 欧洲	歐洲	Ōuzhōu	Europe	p.n.	欧洲动物园有什么动物？(What animals are there in Europe animals area?)

补充词语 Supplementary Vocabulary

Simplified	Traditional	Pinyin	Definition
1. 身份证	身份證	shēnfènzhèng	I.D. (*n.*)
2. 驾驶执照	駕駛執照	jiàshǐ zhízhào	driver's license
3. 护照	護照	hùzhào	passport (*n.*)
4. 狮子	獅子	shīzi	lion (*n.*)
5. 大象	大象	dàxiàng	elephant (*n.*)
6. 猴子	猴子	hóuzi	monkey (*n.*)
7. 袋鼠	袋鼠	dàishǔ	kangaroo (*n.*)
8. 獾	獾	huān	badger (*n.*)
9. 海狸	海狸	hǎilí	beaver (*n.*)
10. 黑熊	黑熊	hēixióng	black bear (*n.*)
11. 海狮	海獅	hǎishī	sea lion (*n.*)
12. 北极熊	北極熊	běijíxióng	polar bear (*n.*)
13. 回家	回家	huí jiā	to return home

沟通任务 Communication Tasks

I Stating what you forgot to mention to someone

我忘了跟_____说_____。

(I forgot to tell _____ that _____.)

Example:

我忘了跟你说我们是学生。

(I forgot to tell you that we are students.)

Practice: Tell a classmate new information you haven't told him or her. Start the sentence with "我忘了跟你说……".

第七课 动物园
Lesson 7 The Zoo

II Asking someone to show their ID

请出示你的_____。

(Please show your _____.)

Examples:

请出示你的<u>学生证</u>。
(Please show your <u>student ID</u>.)
请出示你的<u>身份证</u>。
(Please show your <u>ID</u>.)
请出示你的<u>驾驶执照</u>。
(Please show your <u>driver's license</u>.)
请出示你的<u>护照</u>。
(Please show your <u>passport</u>.)

Practice: Ask your classmate to show you his or her student ID.

III Asking what areas or exhibition halls the zoo has

Question: 请问这家动物园有哪些_____？

(What _____ are there in this zoo?)

Answer: 这家动物园有_____、_____、_____和_____。

(This zoo has _____, _____, _____ and _____.)

Example:

Question 1: 请问这家动物园有哪些<u>区</u>？
(What <u>areas</u> are there in this zoo?)
Answer 1: 这家动物园有<u>非洲动物区、美洲动物区、澳洲动物区和亚洲动物区</u>。
(This zoo has <u>African animals</u>, <u>American animals</u>, <u>Australian animals</u>, and <u>Asian animals areas</u>.)
Question 2: 请问这家动物园有哪些<u>馆</u>？
(What <u>exhibition halls</u> are there in this zoo?)
Answer 2: 这家动物园有<u>大熊猫馆、企鹅馆、海洋馆和鸟类馆</u>。
(This zoo has <u>panda</u>, <u>penguin</u>, <u>aquarium</u>, and <u>birds exhibition halls</u>.)

Practice: Do you know what areas or exhibition hall are there in the nearby zoo? Ask your classmate.

IV) Stating what animals are in which areas or exhibition halls

A single animal: _____在_____。
　　　　　　　　(_____ are in the _____.)
More than one animal: _____、_____和_____都在_____。
　　　　　　　　(_____, _____ and _____ are all in the _____.)

Examples:

棕熊在美洲动物区。
(Brown bears are in the American animals area.)
无尾熊在澳洲动物区。
(Koalas are in the Australian animals area.)
白老虎在亚洲动物区。
(White tigers are in the Asian animals area.)
海豚在海洋馆。
(Dolphins are in the aquarium exhibition hall.)
红鹤在鸟类馆。
(Flamingos are in the birds exhibition hall.)
长颈鹿、斑马和鸵鸟都在非洲动物区。
(Giraffes, zebras, and ostriches are all in the African animals area.)

Practice: In which areas do koalas and white tigers belong in a zoo? Tell the class.

V) Asking which of the places in the zoo is closest to your current location

Question: 哪个地方离我们最近？
　　　　　(Which place is closest to us?)
Answer 1: _____离我们最近。
　　　　　(_____ is closest to us.)
Answer 2: 我不知道。我们查一查地图吧。
　　　　　(I don't know. Let's check the map.)

Example:

Question: 哪个地方离我们最近？
　　　　　(Which place is closest to us?)
Answer 1: 大熊猫馆离我们最近。
　　　　　(The panda exhibition hall is closest to us.)
Answer 2: 我不知道。我们查一查地图吧。
　　　　　(I don't know. Let's check the map.)

Practice: Ask your classmate, "Which ice cream store is closest to us?".

第七课 动物园
Lesson 7 The Zoo

VI Stating what animals one saw in certain places in the zoo

_____在_____看了_____。
(_____ saw _____ in the _____.)

Examples:

我们在非洲动物区看了斑马。
(We saw zebras in the African animals area.)
他在美洲动物区看了棕熊。
(He saw brown bears in the American animals area.)
我在澳洲动物区看了无尾熊。
(I saw koalas in the Australian animals area.)
李小明在亚洲动物区看了白老虎。
(李小明 saw white tigers in the Asian animals area.)
我们在海洋馆看了海豚。
(We saw dolphins in the aquarium exhibition hall.)
张爱华在鸟类馆看了红鹤。
(张爱华 saw flamingos in the birds exhibition hall.)

Practice: What animals did you see in what areas in the zoo? Tell your class.

VII Stating that things that one saw, happened when the person was in a certain place

_____在_____的时候，_____正在_____。
(When _____ was/were in _____, _____ was/were _____.)

Example:

我们在大熊猫馆的时候，两只熊猫正在竹子旁边玩耍。
(When we were in the panda exhibition hall, two pandas were playing next to the bamboo.)

Practice: Tell your classmate what you saw yesterday when you were in Chinese class.

VIII Describing how something or someone is

好_____呀！
(So _____!)

Examples:

好<u>可爱</u>呀！
(So <u>cute</u>!)
好<u>有意思</u>呀！
(So <u>interesting</u>!)
好<u>漂亮</u>呀！
(So <u>good looking</u>!)

Practice: Read aloud the sentences in the example above with a partner. As a class, discuss in what context one would use the sentences.

情景（一） Scenario 1

李小明和张爱华正要一起去动物园。

李小明： 我们要买两张门票。
售票员： 总共三百元。
李小明： 对不起，我忘了跟你说我们是学生了。我们要买学生票。
售票员： 学生票一张120元，两张总共240元。

李小明和张爱华在入口前。

李小明： 爱华，检票口在这儿。我们进去吧。
张爱华： 好，我们走。
检票员： 请出示你们的学生证。谢谢。

李小明和张爱华在动物园里……

张爱华： 你知不知道这家动物园有哪些区？
李小明： 我不知道。我们去游客服务中心问服务员吧。
张爱华： 请问这家动物园有哪些区？
服务员： 这家动物园有非洲动物区、美洲动物区、澳洲动物区和亚洲动物区。
李小明： 请问这家动物园有哪些馆？
服务员： 这家动物园有大熊猫馆、企鹅馆、海洋馆和鸟类馆。

Comprehension Questions

1. 学生票一张多少钱？
2. 动物园有哪些区和哪些馆？

第七课 动物园
Lesson 7 The Zoo

情景(二) Scenario 2

李小明：爱华,你想看哪些动物？

张爱华：我想看长颈鹿、斑马、鸵鸟、无尾熊、海豚、棕熊、白老虎和红鹤。

李小明：长颈鹿、斑马和鸵鸟都在非洲动物区。棕熊在美洲动物区。无尾熊在澳洲动物区。白老虎在亚洲动物区。海豚在海洋馆。红鹤在鸟类馆。你想先去哪个地方？

张爱华：哪个地方离我们最近？

李小明：我不知道。我们查一查地图吧。

Comprehension Questions

1. 张爱华想看哪些动物？
2. 斑马在哪个动物区？
3. 红鹤在哪个馆？

情景(三) Scenario 3

张爱华正在写他的日记……

张爱华的日记

今天我跟李小明去动物园看了很多动物。我们在非洲动物区看了斑马,在美洲动物区看了棕熊,在澳洲动物区看了无尾熊,在亚洲动物区看了白老虎,在海洋馆看了海豚,在鸟类馆看了红鹤。最后我们还去了大熊猫馆看了两只熊猫。我们在大熊猫馆的时候,两只熊猫正在竹子旁边玩耍,好可爱呀！

张爱华

Comprehension Questions

1. 张爱华和李小明去了哪里？
2. 最后张爱华去了哪个馆？看了什么动物？

口语沟通活动 Oral Communication Activities

I. 情况：陈林正在一家他没去过的动物园参观。这家动物园有他想看的动物，但是他不知道这些动物在哪些区和馆。他现在要去问动物园的服务员。

Situation: Chen Lin is visiting a zoo he hasn't been to before. There are particular animals he is interested in seeing, but does not know which areas or exhibition halls they are in. He is going to ask the staff for zoo information.

动物园的资讯　Zoo Information

非洲动物区	长颈鹿 狮子（lion）
亚洲动物区	大象（elephant） 猴子（monkey）
澳洲动物区	无尾熊 袋鼠（kangaroo）
欧洲（Europe）动物区	獾（badger） 海狸（beaver）
美洲动物区	黑熊（black bear） 海狮（sea lion）
北极熊（polar bear）馆	北极熊（polar bear）

任务：两人一组。一个人扮演陈林，另一个人扮演动物园里的服务员。服务员可以用上表所提供的动物园资讯来回答陈林的问题。陈林可以用下方"陈林想看的动物"列表来回答服务员的问题。用下列的会话结构来帮助你做角色扮演。

Task: Work in pairs. One acts as Chen Lin and the other acts as the zoo staff member. The zoo staff member will use the zoo information listed above to answer Chen Lin's questions. Chen Lin will use the "Animals Chen Lin Wants to See" table to answer the staff member's question. Use the conversation structure listed below to help you act out the conversation taken in the zoo.

陈林想看的动物　Animals Chen Lin Wants to See

1. 狮子　　2. 猴子　　3. 袋鼠　　4. 海狸
5. 黑熊　　6. 海狮　　7. 北极熊

会话结构 *Conversation structure:*

陈林：请问这家动物园有哪些区和哪些馆？

第七课 动物园
Lesson 7 The Zoo

服务员: 这家动物园有＿＿＿区、＿＿＿区、＿＿＿区、＿＿＿区、＿＿＿区和＿＿＿馆。

服务员: 你想看哪些动物？

陈林: 我想看＿＿＿、＿＿＿、＿＿＿、＿＿＿、＿＿＿和＿＿＿。

服务员: ＿＿＿在＿＿＿。

＿＿＿在＿＿＿。

＿＿＿在＿＿＿。

＿＿＿在＿＿＿。

＿＿＿和＿＿＿都在＿＿＿。

＿＿＿在＿＿＿。

II. 情况: 中文班的学生正在参观动物园。他们在动物园里两个两个一起走。这些学生们决定他们要从离他们最近的区或馆开始参观(请看以下资讯)。

Situation: The students in the Chinese class are visiting the zoo. They tour around the zoo in pairs. The pairs of students decide that they will visit the area of the zoo which is closest to them (see the information in the table below)

Africa area (非洲动物区) is the closest place to Chen Lin and Li Xiaoming's current location
Asia area (亚洲动物区) is the closest place to Zhang Aihua and Zhang Aiyou's current location
Australia area (澳洲动物区) is the closest place to Lin Mei and Lin Qiang's current location
Europe area (欧洲动物区) is the closest place to Shen Xinyi and Wang Xiaoai's current location
America area (美洲动物区) is the closest place to Li Dapeng and Zhang Li's current location
Polar bear hall (北极熊馆) is the closest place to Chen Peng and Wang Hao's current location
Wu Ailin and Chen Xi are not sure where they are in the zoo. They need to check the map.

任务: 两人一组。用上方表格内的资讯和下方的会话结构做角色扮演。

Task: Work in pairs. Use the information in the table above and the conversation structure below to act out the conversation.

会话结构:

Conversation structure:

陈林: 这家动物园有很多区和很多馆。你想先去哪个地方？

李小明: 哪个地方离我们最近？

陈林：非洲动物区离我们最近。
李小明：我们先去非洲动物区吧。

读写沟通活动 Literacy Communication Activities

1. 王文乐和朋友们计划了几个活动，但是在他妈妈上班前忘了告诉她。王文乐现在正在写小字条让他妈妈知道他的计划，还有他明天才会回家。帮助王文乐用中文完成下列字条。

Wang Wenle has planned several activities with his friends, but forgot to tell his mom before his mom went to work. Wang Wenle is writing notes to let his mom know about his plans and that he won't be back home until tomorrow. Help Wang Wenle complete the notes below in Chinese.

字条一　Note 1
我忘了跟你说_____。
(I want to go shopping with my friends this morning.)

字条二　Note 2
我忘了跟你说_____。
(I want to go hiking with my friends this afternoon.)

字条三　Note 3
我忘了跟你说_____。
(today I won't go home.)
note: use "回家（to return home）" in the sentence

字条四　Note 4
我忘了跟你说_____。
(tomorrow morning I will go home.)
Note: Use "回家" in the sentence.

第七课 动物园
Lesson 7 The Zoo

II. 你的朋友们，林丽、林强和你正在 *QQ* 上讨论你们喜欢哪些运动。你们的对话是用英文写的。与一个同学一起把对话翻译成中文。

Your friends, 林丽, 林强, and you are having a conversation on QQ about what sports you all like to do. The conversation is already written in English. Work with a classmate and translate the conversation into Chinese.

讨论 Discussion

Giant Panda

The giant panda is one of the most precious animals in the world, which has been thought of by many Chinese as an unofficial national symbol. Giant pandas are black and white bears that live in bamboo forests in central China's Sichuan, Shaanxi, and Gansu provinces, which are easily identified with their large black patches around the eyes, ears and on their round bodies. According to the Ministry of Forestry, China currently has about 1,000 giant pandas in the wild. Because of the low number, the giant panda is identified as an endangered species. The Chinese government and the World Wildlife Fund (WWF) are cooperating to save the giant panda by creating panda reserves in China, increasing public awareness about panda conservation, and researching ways to increase their numbers.

Discussion Question:

1. Search online to look for facts about the rare species, giant panda, and report what you find to the class.

Lesson 8

我生病了
I am Sick

沟通任务 Communication Tasks

- Asking what's wrong with someone.
- Suggesting to do certain things immediately.
- Making a diagnosis.
- Explaining the prescription.
- Asking the doctor how to cure an illness.
- Guessing the cause of an illness.
- Wishing that someone gets well soon.

课前讨论 Warm-up Discussion Questions

1. Do you often get sick?
2. Do you usually go to see a doctor when you feel sick?
3. What do you say or do to your family or friends when they are sick?

 生词 Vocabulary

简体 (Simplified)	繁体 (Traditional)	拼音 (Pinyin)	释义 (Definition)	词性 (Parts of speech)	例句 (Examples)
1. 怎么了	怎麼了	zěnmele	what's wrong		你怎么了？(What's wrong with you?)
2. 生病	生病	shēng bìng	to be sick		妈妈生病了。(Mom is sick.)
病	病	bìng	sickness	n.	
3. 赶快	趕快	gǎnkuài	immediately	adv.	我们赶快去学校吧。(Let's go to school immediately.)
4. 带	帶	dài	to bring; to take	v.	我想带你去动物园。(I want to take you to the zoo.)
5. 医生	醫生	yīshēng	doctor	n.	我赶快带你去看医生吧。(Let me take you to see a doctor immediately.)
6. 头痛	頭痛	tóutòng	headache	adj.	我头痛。(I have a headache.)
7. 流鼻涕	流鼻涕	liú bíti	runny nose		我流鼻涕。(I have a runny nose.)
8. 咳嗽	咳嗽	késou	cough	n.	我咳嗽。(I have a cough.)
9. 发烧	發燒	fā shāo	fever		我发烧。(I have a fever.)
10. 并且	並且	bìngqiě	and; used to connect two verb phrases	conj.	你得卧床休息并且保暖。(You have to rest in bed and keep warm.)
11. 无力	無力	wúlì	feel weak		我全身无力。(My whole body feels weak.)
12. 看来	看來	kànlái	to seem like	v.	看来今天会下雨。(It seems like it will rain today.)
13. 得	得	dé	to get	v.	你得病了。(You got sick.)
14. 流行性感冒	流行性感冒	liúxíngxìng gǎnmào	flu		我得了流行性感冒。(I got the flu.)
15. 开药	開藥	kāi yào	to write a prescription		我可以开药给你。(I can write a prescription for you.)

第八课 我生病了
Lesson 8 I am Sick

	药	藥	yào	medicine	n.
16. 药单		藥單	yàodān	prescription	n.	这是你的药单。(This is your prescription.)
17. 餐		餐	cān	meal	n.	我每天吃三餐。(I eat three meals a day.)
18. 饭后		飯後	fàn hòu	after meal		我今天晚饭后想去公园运动。(I want to exercise in the park after dinner today.)
19. 包		包	bāo	dose; a dose of	n. m.w.	我饭后得吃一包药。(I have to take a dose of medicine after a meal.)
20. 记得		記得	jìde	to remember	v.	记得带伞。(Remember to bring an umbrella.)
21. 多		多	duō	many	adj.	记得多喝水。(Remember to drink lots of water.)
22. 休息		休息	xiūxi	to rest	v.	记得休息。(Remember to rest.)
23. 开始		開始	kāishǐ	to start	v.	我今天下午三点开始写中文作业。(I started writing Chinese homework at 3 o'clock this afternoon.)
24. 腹痛		腹痛	fùtòng	abdominal pain	n.	我腹痛。(I have abdominal pain.)
25. 检查		檢查	jiǎnchá	test	n.	现在医生正在做检查。(Now the doctor is doing a test.)
26. 医院		醫院	yīyuàn	hospital	n.	爷爷现在在医院。(Grandfather is in the hospital now.)
27. 结果		結果	jiéguǒ	result	n.	这是你的检查结果。(This is the result of your test.)
28. 急性肠炎		急性腸炎	jíxìng chángyán	intestinal flu		我得了急性肠炎。(I got intestinal flu.)
29. 怎么办		怎麼辦	zěnme bàn	what to do		我现在怎么办？(What do I do now?)
30. 卧床休息		臥床休息	wòchuáng xiūxí	to rest in bed		你得卧床休息。(You have to rest in bed.)
31. 保暖		保暖	bǎonuǎn	to keep warm	v.	你得保暖。(You have to keep warm.)

103

Simplified	Traditional	Pinyin	Definition		Example
32. 禁食	禁食	jìn shí	to fast	v.	我得禁食一天。(I have to fast for a day.)
33. 如果	如果	rúguǒ	if	conj.	如果你生病了,你得去看医生。(If you are sick, you have to go see a doctor.)
34. 病情	病情	bìngqíng	sickness condition	n.	现在你的病情怎么样？(How's your sickness condition now?)
35. 转好	轉好	zhuǎnhǎo	to get better		我的病情转好了。(My sickness condition has gotten better.)
36. 出院	出院	chū yuàn	to be discharged [from the hospital]		我可以出院了。(I can be discharged from the hospital.)
37. 猜	猜	cāi	to guess	v.	我猜我妈妈可能喜欢吃中国菜。(I guess my mother probably likes to eat Chinese food.)
38. 过期	過期	guò qī	to be expired		这杯牛奶过期了。(This glass of milk is expired.)
39. 食物	食物	shíwù	food	n.	我吃了过期的食物。(I ate expired food.)
40. 不管如何	不管如何	bùguǎn rúhé	no matter what		不管如何我希望你的病情转好。(No matter what, I hope your sickness condition gets better.)
41. 早日康复	早日康復	zǎorì kāngfù	to get well soon		祝你早日康复。(I hope you get well soon.)

补充词语 Supplementary Vocabulary

Simplified	Traditional	Pinyin	Definition
1. 病人	病人	bìngren	patient (n.)

第八课 我生病了
Lesson 8 I am Sick

沟通任务 Communication Tasks

I Asking what's wrong with someone

Question: 你怎么了?

or

你哪里不舒服?

(What's wrong with you?)

Answer 1: 我想我可能生病了。

(I think I may have gotten sick.)

Answer 2: 我觉得不太舒服。

(I don't feel very comfortable.)

Elaborated Answer (describing the symptoms):

我_____、_____、_____并且_____。

(I_____, _____, _____, and _____.)

Example:

Question: 你怎么了?

or

你哪里不舒服?

(What's wrong with you?)

Answer 1: 我想我可能生病了。

(I think I may have gotten sick.)

Answer 2: 我觉得不太舒服。

(I don't feel very comfortable.)

Elaborated Answer:

我头痛、流鼻涕、咳嗽、发烧并且全身无力。

(I have a headache, runny nose, cough, fever, and my whole body feels weak.)

Practice: Work in pairs and ask each other "What's wrong with you?". The other should answer, "I think I may have gotten sick."

II Suggesting to do certain things immediately

我赶快_____吧。

(Let me _____ immediately.)

Example:

我赶快<u>带你去看医生</u>吧。

(Let me <u>take you to see the doctor</u> immediately.)

Practice: Tell your classmate, "Let me take you to see the doctor immediately".

III) Making a diagnosis

看来你得了_____。

(It seems that you have _____.)

or

根据_____的结果,你得了_____。

(According to the result of _____, you have _____.)

Examples:

看来你得了<u>流行性感冒</u>。

(It seems that you <u>the flu</u>.)

根据<u>检查</u>的结果,你得了<u>急性肠炎</u>。

(According to the result of <u>the test</u>, you have <u>intestinal flu</u>.)

Practice: Work in pairs. One acts as the patient who says, "I don't feel very comfortable", and the other acts as the doctor who says, "It seems that you have the flu".

IV) Explaining the prescription

这是你的药单。_____吃一包药。还有,记得_____。

(This is your prescription. Take the medicine _____. Also, remember to _____.)

Example:

这是你的药单。<u>每天三餐饭后</u>吃一包药。还有,记得<u>多喝水多休息</u>。

(This is your prescription. Take the medicine <u>three times a day after meals</u>. Also, remember to <u>drink plenty of water and get lots of rest</u>.)

Practice: Read aloud the sentence in the example above to your teacher.

V) Asking the doctor how to cure an illness

Question: 现在怎么办?

(What do we do now?)

第八课　我生病了
Lesson 8　I am Sick

Answer: 现在你需要_____。

(Now you need to _____.)

Example:

Question: 现在怎么办？

(What do I do now?)

Answer: 现在你需要<u>卧床休息、保暖，并且禁食十二个小时</u>。如果明天你的病情转好就可以出院。

(Now you need to <u>rest in bed, keep warm, and fast for 12 hours</u>. If your condition gets better tomorrow you can be discharged.)

Practice: Work in pairs. One asks, "What do I do now?", and the other answers, "Now you need to rest in bed".

VI) Guessing the cause of an illness

我猜是不是_____。

(I am guessing _____.)

Example:

我猜是不是<u>妈妈昨天在家吃了过期的食物</u>。

(I am guessing <u>mom ate expired food at home yesterday</u>.)

Practice: Read aloud the following sentence in Chinese as a class, "I am guessing you ate expired food yesterday".

VII) Wishing that someone gets well soon

我希望_____早日康复。

(I hope _____ will get well soon.)

Example:

我希望<u>妈妈</u>早日康复。

(I hope <u>mom</u> will get well soon.)

Practice: Turn to your neighbor and say, "I hope you will get well soon".

情景（一）Scenario 1

张爱华今天早上不太舒服。

张爱华：我觉得不太舒服。
妈　妈：你怎么了？
张爱华：我想我可能生病了。
妈　妈：我赶快带你去看医生吧。

张爱华和他妈妈在诊所。

医　生：你哪里不舒服？
张爱华：我头痛、流鼻涕、咳嗽、发烧并且全身无力。
医　生：看来你得了流行性感冒。我开药给你。

医生在写药单。

医　生：这是你的药单。每天三餐饭后吃一包药。还有，记得多喝水多休息。
妈妈和张爱华：谢谢医生！

Comprehension Questions

1. 张爱华哪里不舒服？
2. 医生说张爱华得了什么？

情景（二）Scenario 2

李小明的爸爸下课来接他。

李小明：妈妈怎么了？
爸　爸：妈妈今天下午开始腹痛。现在医生正在帮她做检查。我们赶快到医院去看妈妈吧。

李小明和爸爸到了医院。

李小明：医生，请问我妈妈怎么了？
医　生：根据检查的结果，你妈妈得了急性肠炎。
爸　爸：现在怎么办？
医　生：现在她需要卧床休息、保暖、并且禁食12个小时。如果明天她的病情转好就可以出院。

第八课 我生病了
Lesson 8 I am Sick

Comprehension Questions

1. 李小明的妈妈得了什么病?
2. 她现在需要做什么?

情景(三)Scenario 3

李小明正在写他的日记……

李小明的日记

今天妈妈生病了。医生说她得了急性肠炎。我猜是不是妈妈昨天在家吃了过期的食物。不管如何,我希望妈妈早日康复。

Comprehension Questions

1. 李小明的妈妈为什么生病?
2. 李小明希望什么?

口语沟通活动 Oral Communication Activities

I. 情况:下表列出了病人的病症和医生的诊断。

Situation: The following table shows a list of patients' symptoms and the doctor's diagnoses.

病人的病症　**Patients Information**

病人	病症	诊断
病人(patient)一	流鼻涕	流行性感冒
病人二	腹痛	急性肠炎
病人三	咳嗽、发烧	流行性感冒
病人四	腹痛、全身无力	急性肠炎
病人五	头痛	流行性感冒

任务:两人一组。一个人扮演病人,另一个人扮演医生。用下列的会话结构帮助你做角色扮演。

Task: Work in pairs. One acts as the patients and the other acts as the doctor. Use the conversation structure listed below to help you act out the conversation in the hospital.

会话结构:

Conversation structure:

医生:你哪里不舒服?

病人一:我流鼻涕。

医生:看来你得了流行性感冒。我开药给你。

II. 情况:医生诊断后,病人想知道他们的病要怎么治疗,还有他们什么时候可以出院。

Situation: After the diagnoses, the patients want to know how their illness can be cured and when they can be discharged.

病人	怎么治疗	什么时候可以出院
病人一	多喝水多休息	今天晚上
病人二	卧床休息、保暖	明天下午
病人三	禁食十二个小时	后天早上
病人四	禁食六个小时	明天晚上
病人五	多喝水多休息	后天中午

任务:两人一组。一个人扮演病人,另一个人扮演医生。用下列的会话结构帮助你做角色扮演。

Task: Work in pairs. One acts as the patients and the other acts as the doctor. Use the conversation structure listed below to help you act out the conversation in the hospital.

会话结构:

Conversation structure:

病人一:现在怎么办?

医生:现在你需要多喝水多休息。如果今天晚上你的病情转好就可以出院。

第八课 我生病了
Lesson 8 I am Sick

读写沟通活动 Literacy Communication Activities

I. 王文乐是医院里帮医生和说中文的病人做翻译的义工。下列是医生的英文字条。帮王文乐将这些字条在下方空格翻译成中文。

Wang Wenle works as a volunteer in a clinic to help translate the doctor's notes for Chinese speaking patients. Listed below are the doctor's notes in English. Help Wang Wenle to translate them into Chinese in the blanks provided below.

Doctor's Note 1
_____。
(Take the medicine three times a day after meals.)

Doctor's Note 2
记得_____。
(Remember to drink plenty of water and get lots of rest.)

Doctor's Note 3
记得_____。
(Remember to rest in bed and keep warm.)

Doctor's Note 4
记得_____。
(Remember to fast for 24 hours.)

II. 林丽和林强正在QQ上聊林丽的病。他们的对话已写成英文。与一个同学一起把对话翻译成中文。

Lin Li and Lin Qiang are having a conversation on QQ about Lin Li's illness. The conversation is already written in English. Work with a classmate and translate the conversation into Chinese.

我们说中文·中级 1

交谈中请勿轻信汇款、中奖信息、陌生电话，勿使用外挂软件。

林强：你_____？
(What's wrong with you?)

林丽：我觉得_____。
(I don't feel very comfortable.)

林强：我赶快_____吧。
(Let me take you to see the doctor immediately.)

林丽：我看了。根据_____的结果，我得了_____。
(I have seen one. According to the result of the test, I have intestinal flu.)
我猜是不是我昨天吃了_____。
(I am guessing I ate expired food in the restaurant yesterday.)

林强：现在_____？
(What do you do now?)

林丽：现在我需要_____。
(Now I need to fast for 12 hours.)

林强：我希望你_____。
(I hope you will get well soon.)

林丽：谢谢！

第八课 我生病了
Lesson 8 I am Sick

讨论 Discussion

Chinese Medicine

中药 (zhōngyào, Chinese medicine) has been a common part of medical care in China. Chinese people believe that 中药 not only can be used to cure illness and disease, but also to prevent disease and maintain one's well being. The book, 本草纲目 (běncǎo gāngmù) is considered the most comprehensive Chinese medicine book in China, which introduces thousands of plants and animals, and other items that could be used as medicine.

There are hundreds of commonly used 中药 in China. Listed below are a few of them:

1. 人参 (rénshēn, ginseng)
2. 当归 (dāngguī, angelica sinensis)
3. 枸杞 (gǒuqǐ, wolfberry)
4. 黄莲 (huánglián, coptis)

Discussion Question:

1. Work in small groups to research about what illness each of the four 中药 listed above can cure or prevent, or how they keep people healthful.

第九课
Lesson 9

拆礼物
Unwrapping Gifts

沟通任务 Communication Tasks

- Indicating where the presents are.
- Asking if you can start unwrapping presents.
- Describing the present.
- Expressing the excitement of receiving a present.
- Explaining why you gave a certain present to someone.
- Agreeing with someone.
- Asking what present one draws.
- Asking what the present is.

课前讨论 Warm-up Discussion Questions

1. Do you often receive presents? In what occasions?
2. What presents have you given to your family and friends for Christmas? Did they like your gifts?
3. Have you been to a gift exchange party? Did you receive a gift you like in the party? What do you say to express your excitement when you receive a gift you like?

第九课 拆礼物
Lesson 9 Unwrapping Gifts

生词 Vocabulary

简体 (Simplified)	繁体 (Traditional)	拼音 (Pinyin)	释义 (Definition)	词性 (Parts of speech)	例句 (Examples)
1. 圣诞树	聖誕樹	shèngdàn shù	Christmas tree	n.	白色圣诞树很可爱。(White Christmas trees are cute.)
2. 下	下	xià	under	n.	圣诞树下有什么？(What is under the Christmas tree?)
3. 礼物	禮物	lǐwù	gift; present	n.	圣诞树下有很多礼物。(There are many presents under the Christmas tree.)
4. 拆	拆	chāi	to unwrap	v.	我们正在拆礼物。(We are unwrapping presents.)
5. 送	送	sòng	to give [a gift]	v.	我爸爸送我一个圣诞节礼物。(My father gives me a Christmas present.)
6. 圆形	圓形	yuánxíng	round	n.	我的礼物是圆形的。(My present is round shaped.)
7. 包装纸	包裝紙	bāozhuāng zhǐ	wrapping paper	n.	蓝色的包装纸很好看。(The blue wrapping paper looks very nice.)
8. 哇	哇	wa	wow	interj.	哇！太棒了！(Wow! Excellent!)
9. 最近	最近	zuìjìn	recently	n.	我最近开始学中文。(I started to study Chinese recently.)
10. 队	隊	duì	team	n.	我最近加入了篮球队。(I joined the basketball team recently.)
11. 说得对	說得對	shuō de duì	right		你说得对！(You are right!)
12. 方形	方形	fāngxíng	square	n.	我的房子是方形的。(My house is square shaped.)
13. 兴趣	興趣	xìngqù	interest	n.	我很有兴趣学中文。(I have an interest in learning Chinese.)

14. 本	本	běn	classifier for books	m.w.	我很喜欢这本中文书。(I like this Chinese book very much.)
15. 字典	字典	zìdiǎn	dictionary	n.	我的生日礼物是一本字典。(My birthday gift is a dictionary.)
16. 抽	抽	chōu	to draw	v.	谁抽到蓝色的礼物？(Who drew the blue present?)
17. 号	號	hào	number	n.	谁抽到一号礼物？(Who drew present #1?)
18. 前面	前面	qiánmiàn	front	n.	请到前面来拆礼物。(Please come to the front to unwrap the present.)
19. 长条形	長條形	chángtiáoxíng	rectangular	n.	一号礼物是长条形的。(Present #1 is rectangular shaped.)
20. 山水画	山水畫	shān shuǐhuà	landscape painting	n.	我有一张中国山水画。(I have a Chinese landscape painting.)
21. 漂亮	漂亮	piàoliang	beautiful	adj.	这张中国山水画真漂亮！(This Chinese landscape painting is beautiful!)
22. 圣诞节	聖誕節	shèngdàn jié	Christmas holiday (n.)		圣诞节快乐！(Merry Christmas!)
23. 收	收	shōu	to receive (v.)		我收到五个圣诞节礼物。(I received five Christmas presents.)

补充词语 Supplementary Vocabulary

Simplified	Traditional	Pinyin	Definition
1. 长方形	長方形	chángfāngxíng	rectangular (n.)
2. 椭圆形	橢圓形	tuǒyuánxíng	oval (n.)
3. 五角形	五角形	wǔjiǎoxíng	pentagonal (n.)
4. 项链	項鍊	xiàngliàn	necklace (n.)
5. 音乐盒	音樂盒	yīnyuè hé	music box (n.)
6. 太阳眼镜	太陽眼鏡	tàiyáng yǎnjìng	sunglasses

第九课 拆礼物
Lesson 9 Unwrapping Gifts

7. 小说	小說	xiǎoshuō	novel (*n.*)
8. 月历	月曆	yuèlì	calendar (*n.*)
9. 杂志	雜誌	zázhì	magazines (*n.*)
10. 手表	手錶	shǒubiǎo	watch (*n.*)
11. 支	支	zhī	classifier for pens, pencils, and calligraphy brushes (*m.w.*)
12. 毛笔	毛筆	máobǐ	calligraphy brush (*n.*)

沟通任务 Communication Tasks

I) Indicating where the presents are

_____ 有好多礼物。

(There are many presents _____.)

Examples:

<u>圣诞树下</u>有好多礼物。

(There are many presents <u>under the Christmas tree</u>.)

<u>桌子上</u>有一个礼物。

(There is a present <u>on the table</u>.)

Practice: Say the sentence in Chinese aloud, "There are five presents under the Christmas tree!"

II) Asking if you can start unwrapping presents

Question: 我可以开始拆礼物吗？

(Can I start unwrapping the presents?)

Answer: 当然可以。

(Of course you can.)

Example:

Question: 我可以开始拆礼物吗？

(Can I start unwrapping the presents?)

Answer: 当然可以。

(Of course you can.)

Elaborated Answer:

当然可以。你可以先拆我送你的礼物。

(Of course you can. You can unwrap the present I gave you.)

Practice: Ask your teacher as a class, "Can I start unwrapping the presents?"

III) Describing the present

我送你的礼物是_____形的、有_____色包装纸的那个。

(The present I gave you is the _____ shaped one with _____ wrapping paper.)

Examples:

我送你的礼物是<u>圆</u>形的、有<u>蓝</u>色包装纸的那个。

(The present I gave you is the <u>round</u> shaped one with <u>blue</u> wrapping paper.)

我送你的礼物是<u>方</u>形的、有<u>红</u>色包装纸的那个。

(The present I gave you is the <u>square</u> shaped one with <u>red</u> wrapping paper.)

Variation:

一号礼物是<u>长条</u>形的、有<u>绿</u>色包装纸的那个。

(Present #1 is the <u>rectangular</u> shaped one with <u>green</u> wrapping paper.)

Practice: Describe to your classmate the shape and the color of the wrapping paper of the present you most recently gave to a friend.

IV) Expressing the excitement of receiving a present

哇!太棒了!是_____!

(Wow! Great! It is a_____!)

Examples:

哇!太棒了!是<u>一个篮球</u>!

(Wow! Great! It is a basketball!)

哇!太棒了!是<u>一本中文字典</u>!

(Wow! Great! It is a Chinese dictionary!)

Practice: You just received a swimsuit you really like. You want to say in Chinese, "Wow! Great! It is a swimsuit!".

第九课 拆礼物
Lesson 9 Unwrapping Gifts

V) Explaining why you gave a certain present to someone

我知道你最近_____，可能需要常常_____，所以我送你_____。

(I know you recently _____, you probably often need to _____, so I gave you _____ as a gift.)

Examples:

我知道你最近<u>加入了学校篮球队</u>，可能需要常常<u>练习打篮球</u>，所以我送你<u>一个篮球</u>。

(I know you recently <u>joined the school basketball team</u>, you probably often need to <u>practice playing basketball</u>, so I gave you a <u>basketball</u> as a gift.)

我知道你最近<u>很有兴趣学中文</u>，可能需要常常<u>练习中文</u>，所以我送你<u>一本中文字典</u>。

(I know you recently <u>have an interest in learning Chinese</u>, you probably often need to <u>practice Chinese</u>, so I gave you <u>a Chinese dictionary</u> as a gift.)

Practice: Tell a classmate, "I know you recently joined the swim summer camp, you probably often need to practice swimming, so I gave you a swimsuit as a gift."

VI) Agreeing with someone

你说得对！

(You are right!)

Example:

A: 我知道你喜欢听音乐。

(I know you like to listen to music.)

B: 你说得对！

(You are right!)

Practice: Tell a classmate what you know about him or her. Start the sentence with 我知道你……. If you are right, your classmate will answer you with the sentence, "你说得对！".

VII) Asking what present one draws

Question: 谁抽到_____号礼物？请到_____来拆礼物。

(Who drew present #_____? Please come to _____ to unwrap the present.)

Answer: 是我！

(It's me!)

119

Attention:

1. A verb which is followed by 到 emphasizes that the action has taken place. For example, "我看到你" means "I saw you.".

Example:

Question: 谁抽到一号礼物？请到前面来拆礼物。

(Who drew Present #1? Please come to the front to unwrap the present.)

Answer: 是我！

(It's me!)

Practice: Work in pairs. One asks the question listed in the example and the other reads aloud the answer.

VIII) Asking what the present is

Question: 是什么礼物？

(What is the gift?)

Answer: 是_____！

(It is _____!)

Example:

Question: 是什么礼物？

(What is the gift?)

Answer: 是一张中国山水画！

(It is a Chinese landscape painting!)

Practice: Work in pairs. One asks, "What is the gift?", and the other says, "It is a new Chinese dictionary!".

情景(一) Scenario 1

李小明和他的家人正在客厅拆圣诞节礼物。

李小明：圣诞树下有好多礼物。我可以开始拆礼物吗？

妈　妈：当然可以。

爸　爸：你可以先拆我送你的礼物。我送你的礼物是圆形的、有蓝色包装纸的那个。

李小明正在拆一个圆形蓝色包装的礼物。

李小明：哇！太棒了！是一个篮球！

爸　爸：我知道你最近加入了学校篮球队，可能需要常常练习打篮球，所以我送你一

第九课 拆礼物
Lesson 9　Unwrapping Gifts

　　　　个篮球。

李小明：你说得对！谢谢爸爸。
妈　妈：现在你可以拆我送你的礼物。我送你的礼物是方形的、有红色包装纸的那个。

李小明正在拆一个方形红色包装的礼物。

李小明：是一本中文字典！
妈　妈：我知道你最近很有兴趣学中文，可能需要常常练习中文，所以我送你一本中文字典。
妈　妈：你说得对！ 谢谢妈妈。

Comprehension Questions

1. 李小明的爸爸送李小明什么礼物？
2. 李小明的妈妈送李小明什么礼物？

情景(二) Scenario 2

中文班正在举行期末交换礼物派对。王老师一个一个叫抽到号码的学生到教室前拆他们的礼物。

王老师：谁抽到一号礼物？请到前面来拆礼物。
吴家玲：是我！
王老师：一号礼物是长条形的、有绿色包装纸的那个。

吴家玲正在拆一个矩形绿色包装的礼物。

The class: 是什么礼物？
吴家玲：是一张中国山水画！

吴家玲展示了中国山水画给大家看。

The class: 真漂亮。

Comprehension Questions

1. 谁抽到一号礼物？
2. 吴家玲的礼物是什么？

情景(三) Scenario 3

李小明正在写他的日记……

李小明的日记

今天是圣诞节。我收到了爸爸妈妈送我的圣诞节礼物。爸爸送我一个篮球。妈妈送我一本中文字典。这两个礼物我都很喜欢。谢谢爸爸妈妈！

Comprehension Questions

1. 为什么今天李小明收到了礼物？
2. 李小明喜欢他的礼物吗？

口语沟通活动 Oral Communication Activities

I. 情况：今天是王丽的生日。她收到了很多朋友送她的礼物。她正在拆礼物，看看她的朋友们送她什么礼物。下表列出了有关这些礼物的资讯。

Situation: Today is Wang Li's birthday. She received a lot of presents from her friends. She is going to unwrap the presents to find out what her friends gave her. The information about the presents is listed below.

谁送的礼物？	形状	包装纸颜色	什么礼物？
吴爱林	圆形	紫色	一条项链（necklace）
陈林	长方形（rectangular）	粉红色	一个音乐盒（music box）
张喜	椭圆形（oval）	黄色	一顶帽子
王为	五角形（pentagonal）	咖啡色	一副(pair)太阳眼镜（sunglasses）

任务：两人一组。一个人扮演王丽，另一个人扮演王丽的朋友。用表格里的资讯和下方的会话结构做角色扮演。

Task: Work in pairs. One acts as Wang Li and the other acts as Wang Li's friends. Use the information in the table and the conversation structure below to act out the

第九课 拆礼物
Lesson 9　Unwrapping Gifts

conversation.

会话结构:
Conversation structure:

王丽:我可以开始拆礼物吗?

吴爱林:当然可以。你可以先拆我送你的礼物。我送你的礼物是圆形的、有紫色包装纸的那个。

王丽正在拆礼物……

王丽:哇! 太棒了! 是<u>一条项链</u>!

II. 情况:中文班的学生继续在拆礼物。

Situation: The Chinese class continues to unwrap the presents they drew.

任务:分小组练习。一个人扮演王老师,其他人扮演拆礼物的学生。用下方表格里的资讯和会话结构做角色扮演。

Task: Work in small groups. One acts as Wang Laoshi and the rest act as students who unwrap the presents. Use the information in the table and the conversation structure listed below to act out the conversation.

礼物号码	收到礼物的人	礼物
二	林美	一本中文小说(novel)
三	张文中	一本月历(calendar)
四	陈林	一本英文杂志(magazine)
五	王小华	一只手表(watch)
六	林丽	一支(classifier for pens) 毛笔(Chinese brush)

会话结构:
Conversation structure:

王老师:谁抽到二号礼物? 请到前面来拆礼物。

林美:是我!

中文班:是什么礼物?

林美:是<u>一本中文小说</u>!

读写沟通活动 Literacy Communication Activities

I. 李大华看到在他家里的不同地点有很多礼物。在下方空格替李大华描述出这些礼物的位置。

Li Dahua saw a lot of presents placed at different places in his house. Help Li Dahua to indicate the locations of the presents in the blanks provided below.

_____。

(There are many presents under the Christmas tree.)

_____。

(There is a present on the table.)

第九课 拆礼物
Lesson 9　Unwrapping Gifts

_____。

(There are three presents under the table.)

_____。

(There are six presents next to the Christmas tree.)

II. 吴家玲想寄一些礼物到中国给她的朋友们。你的任务是帮吴家玲写中文字条解释她为什么想给她的朋友们这些礼物。

Wu Jialing wants to send several presents to her friends in China. Your task is to help Wu Jialing write notes explaining why she wants to give her friends certain gifts.

字条一　Note 1

我知道你最近加入了_____,可能需要常常_____打
　　　　　　　　　(the school basketball team)　　　　　　　(practice)
篮球,所以我送你_____。
　　　　　　　(a basketball)

125

字条二　Note 2

我知道你最近 _____,可能需要常常练习
　　　　　(have been interested in learning English)
_____,所以我送你一本_____。
 (writing English)　　　　　　　(English dictionary)

字条三　Note 3

我知道你最近加入了_____,可能需要常常_____打
　　　　　　　　　　(the school baseball team)　　　　　　(practice)
棒球,所以我送你_____。
　　　　　　　　　(a baseball)

字条四　Note 4

我知道你最近 _____,可能需要常常练习
　　　　　(have been interested in learning Japanese)
_____,所以我送你一本_____。
 (speaking Japanese)　　　　　　(Japanese dictionary)

讨论 Discussion

Red Envelope

红包 (hóngbāo, red envelope or red packet) is a red envelope used for holding money as a gift during holidays or social occasions. The red color of the envelope symbolizes good luck. It is common to give 红包 on the following occasions: Chinese New Year, weddings, birth of a newborn, promotions, and company celebration events.

The amount of money placed in the envelope usually ends with an even digit. It is common for the amount of 红包 to contain the number, eight, as it is considered a lucky number. On the other hand, the number four should be avoided as the pronunciation of four in Chinese sounds like the word, death.

第九课　拆礼物
Lesson 9　Unwrapping Gifts

Discussion Question:

1. Get into small groups to role play giving out 红包 on different occasions. What do you say in Chinese when you give or receive 红包?

第十课
Lesson 10

新年快乐
Happy New Year

沟通任务 Communication Tasks

- Asking for travel suggestions.
- Asking what other places one wants to visit.
- Pointing out that the distance between two places is not far.
- Suggesting what one can do after a certain event.
- Expressing that you look forward to a trip.
- Asking what performance one will give in New Year celebration.
- Asking what kind of dance one plans to do.
- Asking if there are other activities after performances end.

课前讨论 Warm-up Discussion Questions

1. How do you celebrate the New Year?
2. Have you performed in a New Year celebration event?

第十课 新年快乐
Lesson 10 Happy New Year

生词 Vocabulary

简体 (Simplified)	繁体 (Traditional)	拼音 (Pinyin)	释义 (Definition)	词性 (Parts of speech)	例句 (Examples)
1. 到达	到達	dàodá	to arrive	v.	我们到达中国了。(We arrived in China.)
2. 港口	港口	gǎngkǒu	harbor	n.	纽约港口很大。(New York Harbor is big.)
3. 参观	參觀	cānguān	to visit	v.	昨天，我朋友到我们学校参观了。(My friends visited my school yesterday.)
4. 野餐	野餐	yěcān	to picnic	v.	中午我们可以到中央公园野餐。(We can go picnicing in Central Park at noon.)
5. 俯瞰	俯瞰	fǔkàn	to overlook	v.	我们可以到帝国大厦俯瞰纽约。(We can go to the Empire State Building to overlook New York.)
6. 市	市	shì	city	n.	纽约市很大。(New York City is big.)
7. 景色	景色	jǐngsè	scenery	n.	纽约市的景色很漂亮。(The scenery of New York City is beautiful.)
8. 音乐剧	音樂劇	yīnyuèjù	musical	n.	晚上我们可以去百老汇看音乐剧。(We can go to Broadway to see a musical in the evening.)
9. 倒数	倒數	dàoshǔ	count down	v.	我想去时代广场参加新年倒数。(I want to go to Times Square to join the New Year countdown.)
10. 远	遠	yuǎn	far	adj.	歌剧院离时代广场不远。(The opera house is not far from Times Square.)
11. 期待	期待	qīdài	to look forward	v.	我真期待我的生日派对。(I really look forward to my birthday party.)

12. 次	次	cì	time	m.w.	我真期待这次的圣诞节派对。(I really look forward to the Christmas party this time.)
13. 纽约之旅	紐約之旅	Niǔyuē zhī lǚ	the New York trip		我真期待这次的纽约之旅。(I really look forward to the New York trip this time.)
14. 小组	小組	xiǎozǔ	small group	n.	你们小组有几个人？(How many people are in your small group?)
15. 表演	表演	biǎoyǎn	to perform	v.	我的小组准备表演跳舞。(My small group prepares to give a dance performance.)
16. 打算	打算	dǎsuàn	to plan to	v.	你们打算做什么？(What do you plan to do?)
17. 精彩	精彩	jīngcǎi	wonderful	adj.	你们的表演一定会很精彩。(Your performance will definitely be wonderful.)
18. 希望如此	希望如此	xīwàng rúcǐ	hope so		希望如此。(Hope so.)
19. 花	花	huā	to spend	v.	我们花了很多时间练习中文。(We spent a lot of time practicing Chinese.)
20. 首	首	shǒu	classifier for songs	m.w.	我唱了一首歌。(I sang a song.)
21. 自己	自己	zìjǐ	oneself	pron.	我自己去了中国。(I went to China myself.)
22. 有意思	有意思	yǒuyìsi	interesting		真有意思！(How interesting!)
23. 结束	結束	jiéshù	end	v.	表演结束后你想做什么？(What do you want to do after the end of the performance?)
24. 其他	其他	qítā	other	pron.	中国新年学校有什么其他活动？(What other activities does the school have during Chinese New Year?)
25. 抽奖	抽獎	chōu jiǎng	sweepstake		表演结束后有抽奖活动。(After the performances end, there are sweepstakes.)

第十课 新年快乐
Lesson 10 Happy New Year

简体 (Simplified)	繁体 (Traditional)	拼音 (Pinyin)	释义 (Definition)	词性 (Parts of speech)	例句 (Examples)
26. 非常	非常	fēicháng	very much	adv.	我非常喜欢唱中文歌。(I like to sing Chinese songs very much.)
27. 成功	成功	chénggōng	successful	adj.	我希望我们的表演会很成功。(I hope our performance will be very successful.)

专有名词 Proper Nouns

简体 (Simplified)	繁体 (Traditional)	拼音 (Pinyin)	释义 (Definition)	词性 (Parts of speech)	例句 (Examples)
1. 自由岛	自由島	zìyóudǎo	Liberty Island	p.n.	我们可以去纽约的自由岛。(We can go to Liberty Island in New York.)
2. 自由女神像	自由女神像	Zìyóu nǚshén xiàng	Statue of Liberty	p.n.	我们可以去纽约参观自由女神像。(We can visit the Statue of Liberty in New York.)
3. 中央公园	中央公園	Zhōngyāng gōngyuán	Central Park	p.n.	昨天我们去了中央公园。(We went to Central Park yesterday.)
4. 帝国大厦	帝國大廈	Dìguó dàshà	Empire State Building	p.n.	帝国大厦在纽约。(The Empire State Building is in New York.)
5. 百老汇	百老匯	Bǎilǎohuì	Broadway	p.n.	晚上我们可以去百老汇。(We can go to Broadway in the evening.)
6. 歌剧魅影	歌劇魅影	Gējùmèiyǐng	Phantom of the Opera	p.n.	我们去纽约看歌剧魅影。(We can go see Phantom of the Opera in New York.)
7. 时代广场	時代廣場	Shídài guǎngchǎng	Times Square	p.n.	我想去时代广场。(I want to go to Times Square.)
8. 女神卡卡	女神卡卡	Nǚshén kǎkǎ	Lady Gaga	p.n.	女神卡卡的歌很好听。(Lady Gaga's songs are nice.)
9. 扑克脸	撲克臉	Pūkè liǎn	Poker Face	p.n.	我们打算跳女神卡卡的扑克脸。(We plan to dance to Lady Gaga's *Poker Face*.)

131

我们说中文·中级 1

补充词语 Supplementary Vocabulary

Simplified	Traditional	Pinyin	Definition
1. 中国民俗舞	中國民俗舞	Zhōngguó mínsú wǔ	Chinese folk dance
2. 国际标准舞	國際標準舞	guójì biāozhǔn wǔ	ballroom dance
3. 天生完美	天生完美	Tiānshēng wánměi	*Born This Way* Lady Gaga's song
4. 比赛	比賽	bǐsài	competition (*n.*)
5. 派对	派對	pàiduì	party (*n.*)
6. 演讲	演講	yǎnjiǎng	speech (*n.*)

句型用法 Sentence Structure and Use

I Asking for travel suggestions

Question: 我们到达_____以后要到哪儿旅游？

(After arriving in _____, where do we want to travel?)

Answer: 我们可以_____。

(We can _____.)

Example:

Question: 我们到达<u>纽约</u>以后要到哪儿旅游？

(After arriving in <u>New York</u>, where do we want to travel?)

Answer 1: 我们可以<u>去纽约港口的自由岛上参观自由女神像</u>。

(We can <u>visit the Statue of Liberty on Liberty Island in NewYork Harbor.</u>)

Answer 2: 我们可以<u>坐地铁到中央公园野餐</u>。

(We can <u>take the subway to Central Park to have a picnic.</u>)

Answer 3: 我们可以<u>到帝国大厦俯瞰纽约市的景色</u>。

(We can <u>go to the Empire State Building to overlook the scenery of New York City.</u>)

Answer 4: 我们可以<u>去百老汇看音乐剧——歌剧魅影</u>。

(We can <u>go to Broadway to see the musical—The Phantom of the Opera.</u>)

Practice: Ask a classmate, "After arriving in Beijing, where do we want to travel?".

第十课 新年快乐
Lesson 10 Happy New Year

II) Asking what other places one wants to visit

Question: 你还想去什么地方参观?

(What other places do you want to visit?)

Answer: 我想 _____。

(I want to _____.)

Example:

Question: 你还想去什么地方参观?

(What other places do you want to visit?)

Answer: 我想去时代广场参加新年倒数。

(I want to join the New Year countdown in Times Square.)

Practice: Continue the conversation from the previous practice and ask the same classmate, "What other places do you want to visit?".

III) Pointing out that the distance between two places is not far

_____ 离 _____ 不远。

(_____ is not far from _____.)

Example:

歌剧院离时代广场不远。

(The opera house is not far from Times Square.)

Practice: Think of two locations in your town which are not far away from each other and tell the class.

IV) Suggesting what one can do after a certain event

_____ 完 _____,我们可以 _____。

(After _____, we can _____.)

Example:

看完歌剧魅影,我们可以走路到时代广场参加新年倒数。

(After seeing the Phantom of the Opera, we can walk to Times Square to join the New Year countdown.)

Practice: Suggest to a classmate that after seeing a certain show, you can go to another event.

V. Expressing that you look forward to a trip

我真期待这次的_____之旅。

(I really look forward to the _____ trip.)

Example:

我真期待这次的<u>纽约</u>之旅。

(I really look forward to the <u>New York</u> trip.)

Practice: Are you planning to go to a trip soon? Where is the place you plan to go? Tell the class that you really look forward to the trip.

VI. Asking what performance one will give during the New Year celebration

Question: 你准备在新年庆祝会上表演什么？

(What are you preparing to perform during the New Year celebration?)

Answer: 我准备表演_____。

(My group is preparing to give a _____ performance.)

Example:

Question: 你准备在新年庆祝会上表演什么？

(What are you preparing to perform during the New Year celebration?)

Answer: 我准备表演<u>跳舞</u>。

(I am preparing to give a <u>dance</u> performance.)

Practice: If you need to give a performance during the New Year celebration, what would you prepare? Ask your classmate this question.

VII. Asking what kind of dance one plans to do

Question: 你们打算跳什么舞？

(What kind of dance do you plan to do?)

Answer: 我们打算跳_____。

(We plan to dance to like they did in _____.)

Example:

Question: 你们打算跳什么舞？

(What kind of dance do you plan to do?)

Answer: 我们打算跳<u>女神卡卡的扑克脸</u>。

(We plan to dance to like they did in <u>Lady Gaga's *Poker Face*</u>.)

Lesson 10 Happy New Year
第十课 新年快乐

Practice: If you were going to give a dance performance, what kind of dance would you perform? Ask your classmate this question.

VIII. Asking if there are other activities after performances end

Question: 表演结束后有没有其他活动？

(Are there other activities after the performances end?)

Answer: 有。表演结束后有_____，也有_____。

(Yes, there are. After the performances end, there will be _____ and _____.)

Example:

Question: 表演结束后有没有其他活动？

(Are there other activities after the performances end?)

Answer: 有。表演结束后有<u>新年倒数</u>，也有<u>抽奖活动</u>。

(Yes, there are. After the performances end, there will be a <u>New Year's countdown</u> and <u>sweepstakes</u>.)

Practice: Read aloud the example above as a class.

情景（一）Scenario 1

李小明和张爱华正打算到纽约庆祝新年。

张爱华：小明，我们十二月三十一号到达纽约以后要到哪儿旅游？

李小明：十二月三十一号早上我们可以去纽约港口的自由岛上参观自由女神像。中午我们可以坐地铁到中央公园野餐。下午我们可以到帝国大厦俯瞰纽约市的景色。晚上我们可以去百老汇看音乐剧——歌剧魅影。你还想去什么地方参观？

张爱华：我想去时代广场参加新年倒数。

李小明：歌剧院离时代广场不远。看完歌剧魅影，我们可以走路到时代广场参加新年倒数。

张爱华：太棒了！我真期待这次的纽约之旅。

Comprehension Questions

1. 李小明和张爱华几月几号到达纽约？
2. 李小明和张爱华早上想去哪儿参观？
3. 爱华午夜十二点想看什么？

135

情景(二) Scenario 2

中文班的学生正在讨论他们的新年表演。

王文丽：家玲，你的小组准备在新年庆祝会上表演什么？
吴家玲：我们小组准备表演跳舞。
王文丽：你们打算跳什么舞？
吴家玲：我们打算跳女神卡卡的扑克脸。
王文丽：你们的表演一定会很精彩。
吴家玲：希望如此。我们花了很长时间练习。你们小组打算表演什么？
王文丽：我们打算唱一首我们自己写的歌——新年快乐。
吴家玲：真有意思。
王文丽：表演结束后有没有其他活动？
吴家玲：有。表演结束后有新年倒数，也有抽奖活动。
王文丽：太棒了！希望我们都能抽到大奖！

Comprehension Questions

1. 吴家玲的表演是什么？
2. 王文丽的表演是什么？
3. 表演结束后有什么活动？

情景(三) Scenario 3

吴家玲正在写她的日记……

吴家玲的日记

十二月三十一号我和我的同学们会在新年庆祝会上跳女神卡卡的扑克脸。我们每天都花很长时间练习。我的同学们都非常期待这次的表演。我希望我们的表演会很成功。

吴家玲

Comprehension Questions

1. 吴家玲几月几号有表演？
2. 吴家玲常常花时间练习表演吗？

Lesson 10 Happy New Year
第十课 新年快乐

口语沟通活动 Oral Communication Activities

I. 情况：中文班的学生将要在新年庆祝会上做不同的舞蹈表演。王老师得准备庆祝会的节目册子并查出学生要表演什么舞蹈。

Situation: Students in the Chinese class are going to give different dance performances during the New Year celebration. Wang Laoshi is going to prepare the program brochure and needs to find out what kinds of dances the students are going to perform.

表演者的名字	舞蹈
吴家玲	女神卡卡的扑克脸
王丽	芭蕾舞
吴爱林	中国民俗舞 (Chinese folk dance)
李小明	国际标准舞 (ballroom dance)
陈今	女神卡卡的天生完美 (*Born This Way*)

任务：两人一组。一个人扮演王老师，另一个人扮演学生。用上表内的资讯和会话结构来做角色扮演。

Task: Work in pairs. One acts as Wang Laoshi and the other acts as the students. Use the information in the table and the conversation structure below to act out the conversation.

会话结构：

Conversation structure:

王老师：你准备在新年庆祝会上表演什么？

吴家玲：我准备表演跳舞。

王老师：你打算跳什么舞？

吴家玲：我打算跳女神卡卡的扑克脸。

王老师：你的表演一定会很精彩。

吴家玲：希望如此。

II. 情况：李小明知道新年表演后有其他的活动。下表列出李小明的哪些同学知道新年表演后有什么活动。

Situation: Li Xiaoming knows that after the New Year performances, there are other activities. Each of his classmates listed in the table below knows one of the activities which is going to take place after the performances.

任务：两人一组。一个人扮演李小明，另一个人扮演李小明的同学。用下方表格里的资讯和会话结构做角色扮演。

Task: Work in pairs. One acts as Li Xiaoming and the other acts as Li Xiaoming's classmates who know about the activities after the performances. Use the information in the table and the conversation structure listed below to act out the conversation.

同学	其他活动
林美	新年倒数
王华	唱歌比赛 (competition)
陈林	抽奖活动
林丽	晚餐派对 (party)
李文	中文演讲 (speech) 比赛

会话结构：

Conversation structure:

李小明: 表演结束后有没有其他活动？
林美: 有。表演结束后有<u>新年倒数</u>。

读写沟通活动 Literacy Communication Activities

I. 吉姆有一个刚从中国来的新室友叫李大华。李大华想了解这个城市里有哪些地方可以去，但是他只会看中文。帮助吉姆将下方要给李大华的字条翻译成中文。

Jim has a new roommate, Li Dahua, from China, who just arrived in town a few days ago. Li Dahua wants to know where places are around town, but he only reads Chinese. Help Jim translate the notes about places in town written for Li Dahua in the blanks provided below.

Lesson 10 Happy New Year

_____。

(The school is not far from the park.)

_____。

(The zoo is not far from the gas station.)

_____。

(The hospital is not far from the subway station.)

_____

(The Chinese restaurant is not far from the freeway.)

II. 林丽、张爱林和林强正在QQ上聊他们将要去的纽约之旅。他们的对话已写成英文。与一个同学一起把对话翻译成中文。

Lin Li, Zhang Aihua, and Lin Qiang are having a conversation on QQ about their upcoming New York trip. The conversation is already written in English. Work with a classmate and translate the conversation into Chinese.

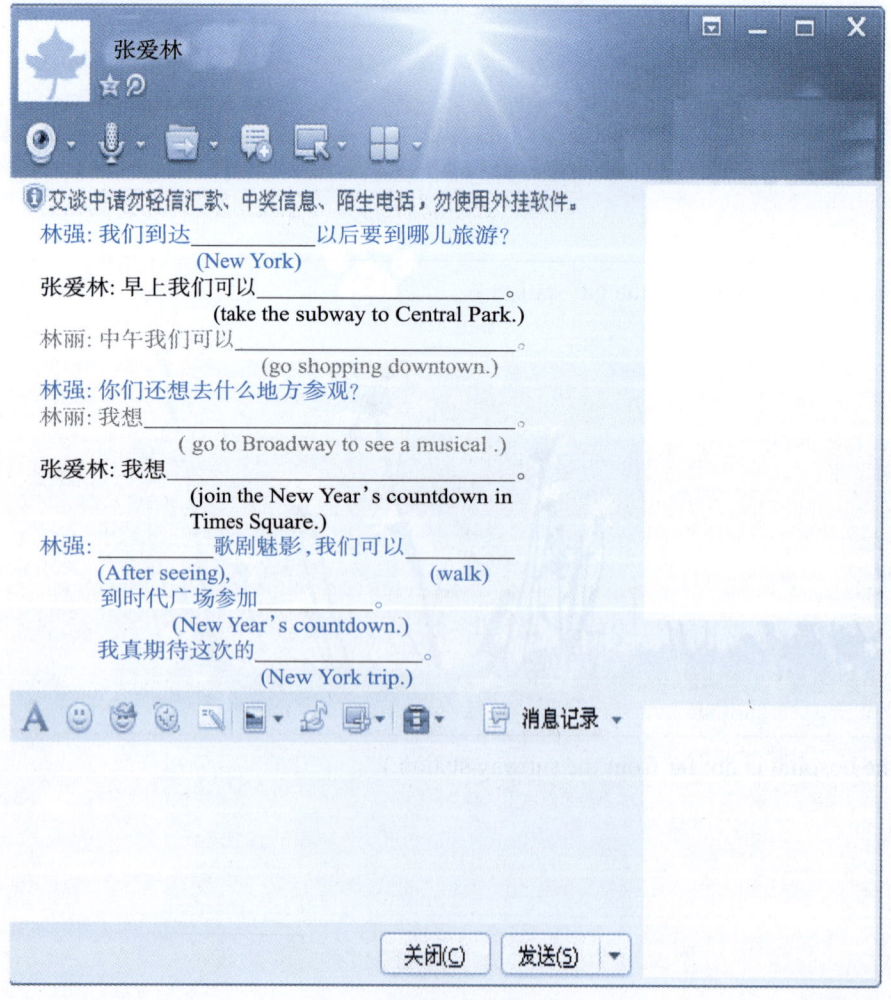

Lesson 10 Happy New Year

 讨论 Discussion

The Lantern Festival

Chinese New Year is the biggest holiday for Chinese people. The celebration lasts for 15 days. The last day of the celebration is called 元宵节 (Yuánxiāo jié, the Lantern Festival). During the Lantern Festival, Chinese people make 元宵 (also called 汤圆, tāngyuán), which are round glutinous rice balls that symbolize family-union. People also hang or carry paper lanterns and get together to play riddle games. A riddle is put on each lantern and people who pick the lanterns try to solve the riddles on the lanterns.

Discussion Question:

1. Do you know any holidays in your country, or other countries, in which people celebrate with their families? What activities do they do? What food do they make?

繁体情景对话课文
Lesson Scenarios in Traditional Chinese Characters

Lesson 1

Scenario 1

李小明、張愛華和吳家玲正要去飯館慶祝李小明的生日。

吳家玲：好久不見！你們暑假過得怎麼樣？
張愛華：我暑假過得很好。我去了加州看我阿姨、姨丈和表弟。我們一起開車去了很多個城市玩。我們去了舊金山、聖地亞哥和洛杉磯。
李小明：我暑假很忙。我每天從早上十點到晚上七點都在中國餐館當收銀員。
吳家玲：你工作做得怎麼樣？
李小明：我的主管說我做得很好。我很高興。家玲，你暑假過得怎麼樣？
吳家玲：我暑假過得不錯。我參加了三個夏令營。我在音樂夏令營學了怎麼吹長笛。我在游泳夏令營學了怎麼游蝶泳和仰泳。我在舞蹈夏令營學了怎麼跳交際舞和芭蕾舞。我學了很多才藝。
張愛華：你可以教我們怎麼跳交際舞嗎？
吳家玲：當然可以。

Scenario 2

王文麗：家玲，你寫完你的中文暑假作業了嗎？
吳家玲：我寫完了。你呢？
王文麗：我還沒有呢。我有一些漢字不會寫。我可以請教你嗎？
吳家玲：當然可以。

王文麗："游泳"的"游"怎麼寫？
吳家玲：我寫給你看。

吳家玲正在教王文麗怎麼寫"游"這個漢字。

王文麗：我還有一個問題。"城市"是什麼意思？
吳家玲："城市"是"city"的意思。
王文麗：最後一個問題，"Thanks for your help"中文怎麼說？
吳家玲："謝謝你的幫助。"
王文麗：家玲，謝謝你的幫助！
吳家玲：不客氣！

Scenario 3
李小明正在寫他的日記……

李小明的日記

今天是學校開學日。上課前我跟我的朋友們聊天。我們聊了暑假做了什麼。張愛華去了加州，吳家玲參加了三個夏令營，我在中國餐館做了收銀員。每個人暑假都過得很好，也很忙。下課後吳家玲教我們怎麼跳交際舞。我們都很開心。今天我很高興再次見到我的朋友們！

Lesson 2

Scenario 1
去年暑假張愛華去加州看他親戚時遇到了一個新的中國朋友李大鵬。

李大鵬：愛華，明天你要不要跟我一起溜滑板？
張愛華：對不起，我明天不能跟你一起溜滑板。我明天早上八點得坐飛機回新墨西哥州。
李大鵬：為什麼你明天要回新墨西哥州？
張愛華：因為我們學校後天開學。我得回學校上課。你呢？你們學校什麼時候開學？
李大鵬：我們學校下星期才開學。
張愛華：真棒！
李大鵬：你離開以前可以給我你的電子郵件地址嗎？我想給你寫電子郵件。
張愛華：當然可以。我們也可以用即時通訊聯絡。
李大鵬：好啊。我還想打電話給你。你可以給我你的手機號碼嗎？
張愛華：當然沒問題。我回新墨西哥州以後想寄一張風景明信片給你，你可以給我你的收信地址嗎？
李大鵬：可以啊。我們把我們的電郵地址、即時通訊地址、手機號碼和收信地址寫在一張紙上吧。

Scenario 2
張愛華和李大鵬正在即時通上聊天。

張愛華：大鵬,你在電腦上看得到我嗎?
李大鵬：我看不到你,因爲我還沒安裝網絡攝像機。
張愛華：你用不用臉書?
李大鵬：用啊。
張愛華：加入我的朋友名單吧。我想給你看我的新照片。

張愛華和李大鵬正在即時通上聊天。

李大鵬：你的朋友名單中有一個人叫李小明。他是我以前的鄰居!
張愛華：真巧!

Scenario 3
李大鵬收到了張愛華的明信片。

親愛的大鵬:
    好久不見! 你好嗎? 你還是每天溜滑板嗎? 你們學校開學了嗎?
    我很想念你。希望我們能常常用即時通訊聊天。
    保持聯絡!

張愛華

Lesson 3

Scenario 1
李小明、張愛華和吳家玲正要去飯館慶祝李小明的生日。

服務員：歡迎光臨。請問幾位?
李小明：三位。
服務員：這邊請。

服務員帶客人到他們的桌子……

服務員：請問這個座位可以嗎?
李小明：可以,謝謝。
服務員：這是菜單。請慢慢看。

五分鐘後……

服務員：請問你們準備好點菜了嗎？
張愛華：我們還需要一點時間。
服務員：沒問題。

五分鐘後……

吳家玲：請問今天的特色菜是什麼？
服務員：今天的特色菜是烤羊排。
吳家玲：我要點一份烤羊排。小明、愛華，你們要點什麼？
李小明：我要點招牌菜——燉牛肉。
張愛華：我吃素，所以我要點一份蔬菜沙拉。
服務員：請問你們需要飲料嗎？
吳家玲：我要一杯汽水。
李小明：我也是。
張愛華：我喝水就好了。
服務員：好，馬上來。

Scenario 2

李小明、張愛華和吳家玲吃完了……

李小明：服務員，我吃不完我的菜。我要打包帶走。
服務員：好。我給你一個盒子。

兩分鐘後……

服務員：這是你們的賬單。
李小明：愛華、家玲，謝謝你們跟我一起慶祝我的生日。今天我請客。
張愛華和吳家玲：真不好意思。謝謝你。

Scenario 3

李小明正在寫他的日記……

李小明的日記

今天是我的生日，我和朋友們一起去了餐厅吃饭，我请客。朋友们，谢谢你们和我一起庆祝生日。

Lesson 4

Scenario 1

李小明的朋友沈心宜要去留學。沈心宜在摩天大樓辦了一個歡送會。李小明想坐地鐵去歡送會，但是他在途中迷路了。李小明正在打電話給他的朋友張愛華求救。

李小明： 餵？請問愛華在嗎？
張愛華： 我就是。
李小明： 我是小明。你知不知道中山地鐵站怎麼走？
張愛華： 對不起，我不知道。你問別人吧。

李小明正找行人問地鐵怎麼走。

李小明： 先生，請問中山地鐵站怎麼走？
路　人： 從這裏直走。過三個紅綠燈以後右轉就到了。
李小明： 謝謝！

李小明終於到了摩天大樓，但是他找不到一樓的電梯。他決定問保安。

李小明： 警衛先生，請問電梯在哪兒？
警衛先生： 往大廳直走。看到維納斯雕像以後左轉就到了。
李小明： 謝謝！

李小明走進電梯裏……

電梯小姐： 請問到幾樓？
李小明： 五十六樓。謝謝。

李小明終於到了歡送會……

沈心宜： 小明，你怎麼這麼晚到？
李小明： 對不起，我迷路了！
沈心宜： 沒關係。歡迎來我的歡送會。

Scenario 2

張愛華和他爸爸要去看一場棒球賽，但是他們在開車到體育場的途中迷路了。

爸爸： 我們停下來問這間加油站的服務員體育場怎麼走吧。

張愛華下車向加油站服務員問路。

張愛華： 請問體育場怎麼走？

服務員：你先上二十八號高速公路。在五號出口下來以後再掉頭就到了。
張愛華：謝謝！

Scenario 3
李小明正在寫他的日記……

李小明的日記

今天晚上我參加了沈心宜的歡送會,但是我迷路了。我找不到中山地鐵站。我也找不到摩天大樓的電梯。別人和警衛先生告訴我怎麼走。最後我終於找到了,但是我也遲到了!

Lesson 5

Scenario 1
王老師正和他的學生們討論他們最喜歡的季節。

王老師：春、夏、秋、冬你們最喜歡哪一個季節?
李小明：我最喜歡夏天,因爲夏天我可以去海邊沖浪,也可以在沙灘玩沙。
張愛華：我最喜歡秋天,因爲秋天我可以慶祝中秋節。我可以跟家人一起吃月餅和賞月。
王文麗：我最喜歡春天,因爲春天我可以看到很多花和蝴蝶。
吳家玲：我最喜歡冬天,因爲冬天我可以慶祝中國新年和元宵節。在中國新年我可以放鞭砲,也可以看舞龍舞獅。在元宵節我可以吃元宵,也可以賞花燈。
李小明：王老師,春、夏、秋、冬,你最喜歡哪一個季節?
王老師：我最喜歡春天。因爲春天的氣候不冷不熱,最舒服。

Scenario 2
張愛華和他媽媽正準備慶祝中秋節。他們在餅店裏買月餅。

媽　　媽：請問這家店的月餅有什麼口味?
店　　員：我們有傳統口味也有新口味。傳統口味的月餅有蓮蓉月餅、豆沙月餅和棗泥月餅。新口味的月餅有綠茶月餅和冰淇淋月餅。
媽　　媽：愛華,你最愛吃哪一種月餅?
張愛華：我最愛吃冰淇淋月餅。
媽　　媽：我們要買兩盒冰淇淋月餅。請問多少錢?
店　　員：總共兩百元。

Scenario 3
王老師正在寫他的日記……

王老師的日記

今天我問了學生們他們最喜歡哪一個季節。有的人喜歡冬天、有的人喜歡夏天、有的人喜歡秋天、有的人跟我一樣喜歡春天。我覺得春天最美麗！

Lesson 6

Scenario 1
李小明和張愛華需要買他們媽媽給他們的購物清單上的東西。

李小明：愛華，你媽媽要你買什麼？
張愛華：我看一下我的購物清單……我媽媽要我買一條魚、一把蔥、四根胡蘿蔔、兩顆洋蔥、一瓶米酒和一瓶蕃茄醬。你呢？
張愛華：我媽媽要我買兩個土豆、一斤火腿、一盒蛋、一袋米和三瓶柳橙汁。
李小明：米很重，我們去找一輛購物車吧。

Scenario 2
吳家玲和她媽媽正要去沃爾瑪買東西。

吳家玲：媽媽，今天我們要去沃爾瑪買什麼？
媽　媽：我們要買一些牛肉，因為明天是你爺爺的生日，我們要烤肉慶祝他的生日。我們還要買一個巧克力生日蛋糕，因為你爺爺最喜歡巧克力口味。

他們到了沃爾瑪……

媽　媽：家玲，請你幫我推一輛購物車。我先到生鮮區買牛肉。
吳家玲：好。

吳家玲的媽媽在生鮮區……

媽　媽：請問還有牛肉嗎？
店　員：對不起，牛肉今天全都賣完了。
媽　媽：什麼時候會進貨？
店　員：可能明天早上十點以後。

繁体情景对话课文
Lesson Scenarios in Traditional Chinese Characters

Scenario 3

吳家玲的媽媽正在寫她的日記……

媽媽的日記

明天是吳家玲爺爺的烤肉生日會。今天我想在沃爾瑪買牛肉和巧克力生日蛋糕,但是沃爾瑪的牛肉全都賣完了。所以今天我先買了巧克力生日蛋糕,明天早上我再去沃爾瑪買牛肉。

Lesson 7

Scenario 1

李小明和張愛華正要一起去動物園。

李小明:我們要買兩張門票。

售票員:總共三百元。

李小明:對不起,我忘了跟你説我們是學生了。我們要買學生票。

售票員:學生票一張一百二十元,兩張總共兩百四十元。

李小明和張愛華在入口前。

李小明:愛華,檢票口在這兒。我們進去吧。

張愛華:好,我們走。

檢票員:請出示你們的學生証。謝謝。

李小明和張愛華在動物園裏……

張愛華:你知不知道這家動物園有哪些區?

李小明:我不知道。我們去遊客服務中心問服務員吧。

張愛華:請問這家動物園有哪些區?

服務員:這家動物園有非洲動物區、美洲動物區、澳洲動物區和亞洲動物區。

李小明:請問這家動物園有哪些館?

服務員:這家動物園有大熊貓館、企鵝館、海洋館和鳥類館。

Scenario 2

李小明:愛華,你想看哪些動物?

張愛華:我想看長頸鹿、斑馬、鴕鳥、無尾熊、海豚、棕熊、白老虎和紅鶴。

李小明:長頸鹿、斑馬、和鴕鳥都在非洲動物區。棕熊在美洲動物區。無尾熊在澳洲動物區。白老虎在亞洲動物區。海豚在海洋館。紅鶴在鳥類館。你想先去哪個地方?

張愛華:哪個地方離我們最近?

李小明：我不知道。我們查一查地圖吧。

Scenario 3
張愛華正在寫他的日記……

張愛華的日記

　　今天我跟李小明去動物園看了很多動物。我們在非洲動物區看了斑馬,在美洲動物區看了棕熊,在澳洲動物區看了無尾熊,在亞洲動物區看了白老虎,在海洋館看了海豚,在鳥類館看了紅鶴。最後我們還去了大熊貓館看了兩只熊貓。我們在大熊貓館的時候,兩只熊貓正在竹子旁邊玩耍,好可愛呀!

Lesson 8

Scenario 1
張愛華今天早上不太舒服。

張愛華：我覺得不太舒服。
媽　媽：你怎麼了?
張愛華：我想我可能生病了。
媽　媽：我趕快帶你去看醫生吧。

張愛華和他媽媽在診所。

醫　生：你哪裏不舒服?
張愛華：我頭痛、流鼻涕、咳嗽、發燒并且全身無力。
醫　生：看來你得了流行性感冒。我開藥給你。

醫生在寫藥單。

醫　生：這是你的藥單。每天三餐飯後吃一包藥。還有,記得多喝水多休息。
媽媽 and 張愛華：謝謝醫生!

Scenario 2
李小明的爸爸下課來接他。

爸　爸：小明,媽媽生病了。
李小明：媽媽怎麼了?
爸　爸：媽媽今天下午開始腹痛。現在醫生正在幫她做檢查。我們趕快到醫院去看媽媽吧。

李小明和爸爸到了醫院。

李小明：醫生，請問我媽媽怎麼了？
醫　生：根據檢查的結果，你媽媽得了急性腸炎。
爸　爸：現在怎麼辦？
醫　生：現在她需要臥床休息、保暖并且禁食十二個小時。如果明天她的病情轉好就可以出院。

Scenario 3

李小明正在寫他的日記……

李小明的日記

今天媽媽生病了。醫生說她得了急性腸炎。我猜是不是媽媽昨天在家吃了過期的食物。不管如何，我希望媽媽早日康復。

Lesson 9

Scenario 1

李小明和他的家人正在客廳拆聖誕節禮物。

李小明：聖誕樹下有好多禮物。我可以開始拆禮物嗎？
媽　媽：當然可以。
爸　爸：你可以先拆我送你的禮物。我送你的禮物是圓形的、有藍色包裝紙的那個。

李小明正在拆一個圓形藍色包裝的禮物。

李小明：哇！太棒了！是一個籃球！
爸　爸：我知道你最近加入了學校籃球隊，可能需要常常練習打籃球，所以我送你一個籃球。
李小明：你説得對！謝謝爸爸。
媽　媽：現在你可以拆我送你的禮物。我送你的禮物是方形的、有紅色包裝紙的那個。

李小明正在拆一個方形紅色包裝的禮物。

李小明：是一本中文字典！
媽　媽：我知道你最近很有興趣學中文，可能需要常常練習中文，所以我送你一本中文字典。
媽　媽：你説得對！謝謝媽媽。

Scenario 2

中文班正在舉行期末交換禮物派對。王老師一個一個叫抽到號碼的學生到教室前拆他們的禮物。

王老師：誰抽到一號禮物？請到前面來拆禮物。
吳家玲：是我！
王老師：一號禮物是長條形的、有綠色包裝紙的那個。

吳家玲正在拆一個矩形綠色包裝的禮物。

The class：是什麼禮物？
吳 家 玲：是一張中國山水畫！

吳家玲展示了中國山水畫給大家看。

The class：真漂亮。

Scenario 3

李小明正在寫他的日記……

李小明的日記

　　今天是聖誕節。我收到了爸爸媽媽送我的聖誕節禮物。爸爸送我一個籃球。媽媽送我一本中文字典。這兩個禮物我都很喜歡。謝謝爸爸媽媽！

Lesson 10

Scenario 1

李小明和張愛華正打算到紐約慶祝新年。

張愛華：小明，我們十二月三十一號到達紐約以後要到哪兒旅遊？
李小明：十二月三十一號早上我們可以去紐約港口的自由島上參觀自由女神像。中午我們可以坐地鐵到中央公園野餐。下午我們可以到帝國大廈俯瞰紐約市的景色。晚上我們可以去百老匯看音樂劇——歌劇魅影。你還想去什麼地方參觀？
張愛華：我想去時代廣場參加新年倒數。
李小明：歌劇院離時代廣場不遠。看完歌劇魅影，我們可以走路到時代廣場參加新年倒數。
張愛華：太棒了！我真期待這次的紐約之旅。

Scenario 2

中文班的學生正在討論他們的新年表演。

王文麗：家玲,你們小組準備在新年慶祝會上表演什麼?
吳家玲：我們小組準備表演跳舞。
王文麗：你們打算跳什麼舞?
吳家玲：我們打算跳女神卡卡的撲克臉。
王文麗：你們的表演一定會很精彩。
吳家玲：希望如此。我們花了很長時間練習。你們小組打算表演什麼?
王文麗：我們打算唱一首我們自己寫的歌——新年快樂。
吳家玲：真有意思。
王文麗：表演結束後有沒有其他活動?
吳家玲：有。表演結束後有新年倒數,也有抽獎活動。
王文麗：太棒了! 希望我們都能抽到大獎!

Scenario 3

吳家玲正在寫她的日記……

吳家玲的日記

　　十二月三十一號我和我的同學們會在新年慶祝會上跳女神卡卡的撲克臉。我們每天都花很長時間練習。我的同學們都非常期待這次的表演。我希望我們的表演會很成功。

词汇表
*Vocabulary Glossary

A					
简体 (Simplified)	繁体 (Traditional)	拼音 (Pinyin)	释义 (Definition)	词性 (Parts of speech)	Lesson
安装	安裝	ānzhuāng	to set up	v.	2

B					
简体 (Simplified)	繁体 (Traditional)	拼音 (Pinyin)	释义 (Definition)	词性 (Parts of speech)	Lesson
芭蕾舞	芭蕾舞	bālěiwǔ	ballet	n.	1
把	把	bǎ	classifier for anything that can be held in one's hand	m.w.	6
白老虎	白老虎	bái lǎohǔ	white tiger	n.	7
斑马	斑馬	bānmǎ	zebra	n.	7
棒	棒	bàng	excellent	adj.	2
包	包	bāo	dose; a dose of	n; m.w.	8
包装纸	包裝紙	bāozhuāng zhǐ	wrapping paper	n.	9
保持	保持	bǎochí	to keep	v.	2
保暖	保暖	bǎonuǎn	to keep warm	v.	8
杯	杯	bēi	a classifier for cups/glasses	m.w.	3

*词汇表中的词汇为每课的生词,不包括专有名词和补充词语。

简体 (Simplified)	繁体 (Traditional)	拼音 (Pinyin)	释义 (Definition)	词性 (Parts of speech)	Lesson
本	本	běn	classifier for books	m.w.	9
表演	表演	biǎoyǎn	to perform	v.	10
冰淇淋	冰淇淋	bīngqílín	ice cream	n.	5
并且	並且	bìngqiě	and: used to connect two verb phrases	conj.	8
病	病	bìng	sickness	n.	8
病情	病情	bìngqíng	sickness condition	n.	8
不错	不錯	búcuò	not bad; pretty good	adj.	1
不管如何	不管如何	bùguǎn rúhé	no matter what		8
不好意思	不好意思	bù hǎoyìsi	embarrassed		3

C

简体 (Simplified)	繁体 (Traditional)	拼音 (Pinyin)	释义 (Definition)	词性 (Parts of speech)	Lesson
猜	猜	cāi	to guess	v.	8
才艺	才藝	cáiyì	talent; skill	n.	1
菜单	菜單	càidān	menu	n.	3
参观	參觀	cānguān	to visit	v.	10
餐	餐	cān	meal	n.	8
查	查	chá	to check	v.	7
拆	拆	chāi	to unwrap	v.	9
长笛	長笛	chángdí	flute	n.	1
长颈鹿	長頸鹿	chángjǐnglù	giraffe	n.	7
长条形	長條形	chángtiáoxíng	rectangular	n.	9
常常	常常	chángcháng	often	adv.	2
成功	成功	chénggōng	successful	adj.	10
城市	城市	chéngshì	city	n.	1
吃素	吃素	chīsù	to be a vegetarian	v.	3
冲浪	沖浪	chōng làng	to surf		5
抽	抽	chōu	to draw	v.	9
抽奖	抽獎	chōu jiǎng	sweepstake		10
出口	出口	chūkǒu	exit	n.	4

简体	繁体	拼音	释义	词性	Lesson
出示	出示	chūshì	to show	v.	7
出院	出院	chū yuàn	to be discharged [from the hospital]		8
传统	傳統	chuántǒng	traditional	adj.	5
春天	春天	chūntiān	spring	n.	5
次	次	cì	time	m.w.	10
从……到……	從……到……	cóng...dào...	from...to...		1
葱	蔥	cōng	spring onion	n.	6

D

简体 (Simplified)	繁体 (Traditional)	拼音 (Pinyin)	释义 (Definition)	词性 (Parts of speech)	Lesson
打包	打包	dǎ bāo	to pack up	v.o.	3
打算	打算	dǎsuàn	to plan to	v.	10
大厅	大廳	dàtīng	hall	n.	4
大熊猫	大熊貓	dàxióngmāo	giant panda	n.	7
带	帶	dài	to bring; to take	v.	8
带走	帶走	dàizǒu	to take away		3
袋	袋	dài	bag	n.	6
蛋糕	蛋糕	dàngāo	cake	n.	6
当然	當然	dāngrán	of course	adv.	1
倒数	倒數	dàoshǔ	count down	v.	10
到达	到達	dàodá	to arrive	v.	10
得	得	dé	to get	v.	8
地方	地方	dìfang	place	n.	7
地铁站	地鐵站	dìtiězhàn	subway station	n.	4
地图	地圖	dìtú	map	n.	7
地址	地址	dìzhǐ	address	n.	2
点菜	點菜	diǎn cài	to order food		3
电梯	電梯	diàntī	elevator	n.	4
电子邮件	電子郵件	diànzǐyóujiàn	e-mail		2
雕像	雕像	diāoxiàng	statue	n.	4
掉头	掉头	diào tuó	to make an U- turn		4
蝶泳	蝶泳	diéyǒng	butterfly stroke	n.	1

Vocabulary Glossary

简体	繁体	拼音	释义	词性	Lesson
冬天	冬天	dōngtiān	winter	n.	5
动物园	動物園	dòngwùyuán	zoo	n.	7
豆沙	豆沙	dòushā	red bean	n.	5
队	隊	duì	team	n.	9
炖牛肉	燉牛肉	dùnniúròu	beef stew		3
多	多	duō	many	adj.	8

F

简体 (Simplified)	繁体 (Traditional)	拼音 (Pinyin)	释义 (Definition)	词性 (Parts of speech)	Lesson
发烧	發燒	fā shāo	fever		8
蕃茄酱	蕃茄醬	fānqiéjiàng	ketchup	n.	6
饭后	飯後	fàn hòu	after meal		8
方形	方形	fāngxíng	square	n.	9
放	放	fàng	to set off	v.	5
飞机	飛機	fēijī	airplane	n.	2
非常	非常	fēicháng	very much	adv.	10
份	份	fèn	(an) order	m.w.	3
风景	風景	fēngjǐng	scenery	n.	2
服务员	服務員	fúwùyuán	service personnel	n.	3
俯瞰	俯瞰	fǔkàn	to overlook	v.	10
腹痛	腹痛	fùtòng	abdominal pain	n.	8

G

简体 (Simplified)	繁体 (Traditional)	拼音 (Pinyin)	释义 (Definition)	词性 (Parts of speech)	Lesson
赶快	趕快	gǎnkuài	immediately	adv.	8
港口	港口	gǎngkǒu	harbor	n.	10
高速公路	高速公路	gāosù gōnglù	freeway		4
告诉	告訴	gàosu	to tell	v.	4
根	根	gēn	classifier for long objects	m.w.	6
跟……一样……	跟……一樣……	gēn...yíyàng...	same as ...		5

简体	繁体	拼音	释义	词性	Lesson
购物	購物	gòu wù	to shop		6
购物车	購物車	gòuwùchē	shopping cart	*n.*	6
馆	舘	guǎn	exhibition hall	*n.*	7
过	過	guò	to spend	*v.*	1
过	過	guò	to pass	*v.*	4
过期	過期	guò qī	to be expired		8

H

简体 *(Simplified)*	繁体 *(Traditional)*	拼音 *(Pinyin)*	释义 *(Definition)*	词性 *(Parts of speech)*	Lesson
海边	海邊	hǎibiān	by the sea; at the beach; used to describe activities in or by the sea		5
海豚	海豚	hǎitún	dolphin	*n.*	7
海洋	海洋	hǎiyáng	sea	*n.*	7
好了	好了	hǎo le	I am fine with just...		3
号	號	hào	number	*n.*	9
号码	號碼	hàomǎ	number	*n.*	2
盒	盒	hé	box	*m.w.*	5
盒子	盒子	hézi	box	*n.*	3
红鹤	紅鶴	hónghè	flamingo	*n.*	7
红绿灯	紅綠燈	hónglǜdēng	traffic light	*n.*	4
后	後	hòu	after	*n.*	1
胡萝卜	胡蘿蔔	húluóbo	carrot	*n.*	6
蝴蝶	蝴蝶	húdié	butterfly	*n.*	5
花	花	huā	flower	*n.*	5
花	花	huā	to spend	*v.*	10
欢送会	歡送會	huānsòng huì	farewell party	*n.*	4
欢迎光临	歡迎光臨	huānyíng guānglín	welcome		3
还	還	hái	still	*adv.*	1
回	回	huí	to return	*v.*	2
火腿	火腿	huǒtuǐ	ham	*n.*	6

Vocabulary Glossary

J

简体 (Simplified)	繁体 (Traditional)	拼音 (Pinyin)	释义 (Definition)	词性 (Parts of speech)	Lesson
即时通讯	即時通訊	jíshí tōngxùn	instant messenger		2
急性肠炎	急性腸炎	jíxìng chángyán	intestinal flu		8
几	幾	jǐ	how many	pron.	3
记得	記得	jìde	to remember	v.	8
季节	季節	jìjié	season	n.	5
寄	寄	jì	to send	v.	2
加入	加入	jiārù	to join	v.	2
加油站	加油站	jiāyóuzhàn	gas station	n.	4
间	間	jiān	classifier for rooms and buildings	m.w.	4
检查	檢查	jiǎnchá	test	n.	8
检票口	檢票口	jiǎnpiàokǒu	ticket checking entrance	n.	7
见到	見到	jiàndào	to see (people)	v.	1
奖	獎	jiǎng	prize	n.	10
交际舞	交際舞	jiāojìwǔ	ballroom dance	n.	1
结果	結果	jiéguǒ	result	n.	8
结束	結束	jiéshù	end	v.	10
斤	斤	jīn	pound	m.w.	6
近	近	jìn	close	adj.	7
进货	進貨	jìn huò	to restock		6
进去	進去	jìnqù	to enter	v.	7
禁食	禁食	jìn shí	to fast	v.	8
精彩	精彩	jīngcǎi	wonderful	adj.	10
景色	景色	jǐngsè	scenery	n.	10
警卫	警衛	jǐngwèi	security guard	n.	4
就	就	jiù	right away	adv.	4

K

简体 (Simplified)	繁体 (Traditional)	拼音 (Pinyin)	释义 (Definition)	词性 (Parts of speech)	Lesson
开始	開始	kāishǐ	to start	v.	8
开心	開心	kāixīn	happy	adj.	1
开学日	開學日	kāixuérì	school start date	n.	1
开药	開藥	kāi yào	to write a prescription		8
看不到	看不到	kàn bú dào	to be unable to see		2
看得到	看得到	kàn de dào	to be able to see		2
看来	看來	kànlái	to seem like	v.	8
烤肉	烤肉	kǎo ròu	to barbeque		6
烤羊排	烤羊排	kǎoyángpái	roasted lamb chop		3
颗	顆	kē	classifier for small spheres	m.w.	6
咳嗽	咳嗽	késou	cough	n.	8
可爱	可愛	kě'ài	cute	adj.	7
可能	可能	kěnéng	possibly	adv.	6
可以	可以	kěyǐ	can	aux.	3
口味	口味	kǒuwèi	flavor	n.	5

L

简体 (Simplified)	繁体 (Traditional)	拼音 (Pinyin)	释义 (Definition)	词性 (Parts of speech)	Lesson
离	離	lí	from	prep.	7
离开	離開	líkāi	to leave	v.	2
礼物	禮物	lǐwù	gift; present	n.	9
莲蓉	蓮蓉	liánróng	lotus seed	n.	5
联络	聯絡	liánluò	to contact	v.	2
脸书	臉書	liǎnshū	Facebook	n.	2
辆	輛	liàng	classifier for carts	m.w.	6
聊天	聊天	liáo tiān	to chat		1
邻居	鄰居	línjū	neighbor	n.	2
溜	溜	liū	to skate	v.	2

简体 (Simplified)	繁体 (Traditional)	拼音 (Pinyin)	释义 (Definition)	词性 (Parts of speech)	Lesson
流鼻涕	流鼻涕	liú bíti	runny nose		8
流行性感冒	流行性感冒	liúxíngxìng gǎnmào	flu		8
柳橙汁	柳橙汁	liǔchéngzhī	orange juice	n.	6

M

简体 (Simplified)	繁体 (Traditional)	拼音 (Pinyin)	释义 (Definition)	词性 (Parts of speech)	Lesson
马上	馬上	mǎshàng	immediately	adv.	3
慢慢	慢慢	mànman	slowly	adj.	3
没问题	沒問題	méi wèntí	no problem		3
每	每	měi	every	pron.	1
美丽	美麗	měilì	beautiful	adj.	5
门票	門票	ménpiào	ticket	n.	7
迷路	迷路	mí lù	to get lost on the road		4
米	米	mǐ	rice	n.	6
米酒	米酒	mǐjiǔ	rice wine	n.	6
名单	名單	míngdān	list	n.	2
明信片	明信片	míngxìnpiàn	postcard	n.	2
摩天大楼	摩天大樓	mótiāndàlóu	skyscraper		4

N

简体 (Simplified)	繁体 (Traditional)	拼音 (Pinyin)	释义 (Definition)	词性 (Parts of speech)	Lesson
哪些	哪些	nǎxiē	which	pron.	7
鸟类	鳥類	niǎolèi	birds	n.	v
纽约之旅	紐約之旅	Niǔyuē zhī lǚ	the New York trip		10

P

简体 (Simplified)	繁体 (Traditional)	拼音 (Pinyin)	释义 (Definition)	词性 (Parts of speech)	Lesson
旁边	旁邊	pángbiān	near by position	n.	7
漂亮	漂亮	piàoliang	beautiful	adj.	9
瓶	瓶	píng	bottle	n.	6

Q

简体 (Simplified)	繁体 (Traditional)	拼音 (Pinyin)	释义 (Definition)	词性 (Parts of speech)	Lesson
期待	期待	qīdài	to look forward	v.	10
其他	其他	qítā	other	pron.	10
企鹅	企鵝	qǐ'é	penguin	n.	7
气候	氣候	qìhòu	climate	n.	5
前	前	qián	before	n.	1
前面	前面	qiánmiàn	front	n.	9
巧	巧	qiǎo	such a coincidence		2
清单	清單	qīngdān	list	n.	6
请教	請教	qǐngjiào	to ask	v.	1
请客	請客	qǐng kè	to treat someone to a meal		3
秋天	秋天	qiūtiān	autumn	n.	5
区	區	qū	area	n.	7
全	全	quán	all	adv.	6

R

简体 (Simplified)	繁体 (Traditional)	拼音 (Pinyin)	释义 (Definition)	词性 (Parts of speech)	Lesson
日记	日記	rìjì	diary	n.	1
如果	如果	rúguǒ	if	conj.	8

S

简体 (Simplified)	繁体 (Traditional)	拼音 (Pinyin)	释义 (Definition)	词性 (Parts of speech)	Lesson
沙滩	沙灘	shātān	beach	n.	5
山水画	山水畫	shānshuǐhuà	landscape painting	n.	9
赏	賞	shǎng	to appreciate	v.	5
赏月	賞月	shǎng yuè	to see and appreciate the Moon		5

Vocabulary Glossary

上	上	shàng	on	n.	2
生病	生病	shēng bìng	to be sick		8
生鲜区	生鮮區	shēngxiān qū	raw food section	n.	6
圣诞节	聖誕節	shèngdànjié	Christmas holiday	n.	9
圣诞树	聖誕樹	shèngdàn shù	Christmas tree	n.	9
食物	食物	shíwù	food	n.	8
市	市	shì	city	n.	10
收	收	shōu	to receive	v.	9
手机	手機	shǒujī	cell phone	n.	2
首	首	shǒu	classifier for songs	m.w.	10
舒服	舒服	shūfu	comfortable	adj.	5
说得对	說得對	shuō de duì	right		9
送	送	sòng	to give [a gift]	v.	9

T

简体 (Simplified)	繁体 (Traditional)	拼音 (Pinyin)	释义 (Definition)	词性 (Parts of speech)	Lesson
特色菜	特色菜	tèsècài	special dish	n.	3
体育场	體育場	tǐyùchǎng	stadium	n.	4
条	條	tiáo	classifier for fish	m.w.	6
停	停	tíng	to stop	v.	4
头痛	頭痛	tóutòng	headache	adj.	8
土豆	土豆	tǔdòu	potato	n.	6
推	推	tuī	to push	v.	6
鸵鸟	鴕鳥	tuóniǎo	ostrich	n.	7

W

简体 (Simplified)	繁体 (Traditional)	拼音 (Pinyin)	释义 (Definition)	词性 (Parts of speech)	Lesson
哇	哇	wa	wow	interj.	9
完	完	wán	to finish	v.	3
玩	玩	wán	to travel	v.	1
玩耍	玩耍	wánshuǎ	to play	v.	7

简体	繁体	拼音	释义	词性	Lesson
晚	晚	wǎn	to be late	*adj.*	4
网络摄像机	網絡攝像機	wǎngluò shèxiàngjī	webcam		2
往	往	wǎng	toward	*prep.*	4
为什么	為什麼	wèi shénme	why		2
位	位	wèi	classifier for persons	*mw.*	3
卧床休息	臥床休息	wòchuáng xiūxí	to rest in bed		8
无力	無力	wúlì	feel weak		8
无尾熊	無尾熊	wúwěixióng	koala	*n.*	7
舞龙舞狮	舞龍舞獅	wǔ lóng wǔ shī	dragon and lion dance		5

X

简体 (Simplified)	繁体 (Traditional)	拼音 (Pinyin)	释义 (Definition)	词性 (Parts of speech)	Lesson
希望如此	希望如此	xīwàng rúcǐ	hope so		10
下	下	xià	under	*n.*	9
下课	下課	xià kè	class dismissed		1
下来	下來	xiàlái	to get off	*v.*	4
下星期	下星期	xià xīngqí	next week		2
夏天	夏天	xiàtiān	summer	*n.*	5
想念	想念	xiǎngniàn	to miss someone	*v.*	2
小组	小組	xiǎozǔ	small group	*n.*	10
兴趣	興趣	xìngqù	interest	*n.*	9
休息	休息	xiūxi	to rest	*v.*	8
学生票	學生票	xuéshēng-piào	student ticket	*n.*	7
学生证	學生證	xuéshēng-zhèng	student ID	*n.*	7

Y

简体 (Simplified)	繁体 (Traditional)	拼音 (Pinyin)	释义 (Definition)	词性 (Parts of speech)	Lesson
洋葱	洋蔥	yángcōng	onion	*n.*	6

词汇表
Vocabulary Glossary

简体	繁体	拼音	释义	词性	Lesson
仰泳	仰泳	yǎngyǒng	back stroke	n.	1
药	藥	yào	medicine	n.	8
药单	藥單	yàodān	prescription	n.	8
野餐	野餐	yěcān	to picnic	v.	10
一点	一點	yìdiǎn	a little	num.	3
一些	一些	yīxiē	some	num.	1
医生	醫生	yīshēng	doctor	n.	8
医院	醫院	yīyuàn	hospital	n.	8
以后	以後	yǐhòu	in the future	n.	2
以前	以前	yǐqián	before; in the past	n.	2
意思	意思	yìsi	meaning	n.	1
音乐剧	音樂劇	yīnyuèjù	musical	n.	10
用	用	yòng	to use	v.	2
游客服务中心	遊客服務中心	yóukè fúwù zhōngxīn	tourist information center		7
有的	有的	yǒude	some	pron.	5
有意思	有意思	yǒuyìsi	interesting		10
右转	右轉	yòu zhuǎn	to turn right		4
鱼	魚	yú	fish	n.	6
元宵	元宵	yuánxiāo	glutinous rice ball	n.	5
圆形	圓形	yuánxíng	round	n.	9
远	遠	yuǎn	far	adj.	10
月饼	月餅	yuèbing	moon cake	n.	5

Z

简体 (Simplified)	繁体 (Traditional)	拼音 (Pinyin)	释义 (Definition)	词性 (Parts of speech)	Lesson
再次	再次	zàicì	again	adv.	1
早日康复	早日康復	zǎorì kāngfù	to get well soon		8
枣泥	棗泥	zǎoní	jujube	n.	5
怎么办	怎麼辦	zěnme bàn	what to do		8
怎么了	怎麼了	zěnmele	what's wrong		8
张	張	zhāng	classifier for thin pieces	m.w.	2
账单	賬單	zhàngdān	bill	n.	3

招牌菜	招牌菜	zhāopái cài	signature dish; a dish that a restaurant is well known for	*n.*	3
找不到	找不到	zhǎobùdào	cannot find		4
找到	找到	zhǎodào	to find		4
这	這	zhè	this	*pron.*	3
这边	這邊	zhè biān	this way		3
这里	這裡	zhèlǐ	here	*pron.*	4
这么	這麼	zhème	so	*pron.*	4
真	真	zhēn	really	*adv.*	2
正在	正在	zhèngzài	in the process of	*prep.*	7
直走	直走	zhí zǒu	go straight		4
只	隻	zhī	classifier for animals	*m.w.*	7
纸	紙	zhǐ	paper	*n.*	2
终于	終於	zhōngyú	eventually; finally	*adv.*	4
重	重	zhòng	heavy	*adj.*	6
竹子	竹子	zhúzi	bamboo	*n.*	7
主管	主管	zhǔguǎn	supervisor	*n.*	1
转好	轉好	zhuǎnhǎo	to get better		8
准备	準備	zhǔnbèi	to prepare	*v.*	3
字典	字典	zìdiǎn	dictionary	*n.*	9
自己	自己	zìjǐ	oneself	*pron.*	10
棕熊	棕熊	zōngxióng	brown bear	*n.*	7
总共	總共	zǒnggòng	in total	*adv.*	5
最	最	zuì	the most	*adv.*	5
最后	最後	zuìhòu	final; last	*n.*	1
最近	最近	zuìjìn	recently	*n.*	9
左转	左轉	zuǒ zhuǎn	to turn left		
座位	座位	zuòwèi	seat	*n.*	3

我们说中文
We Speak Chinese

练习册　中级1
Workbook　Intermediate 1

宋可音（Ko-Yin Sung）　编著

目录 Contents

第一课	你暑假过得怎么样？	1
Lesson 1	How Did Your Summer Vacation Go?	
第二课	我们保持联络！	5
Lesson 2	Let's Keep in Touch!	
第三课	你们准备好点菜了吗？	9
Lesson 3	Are You Ready to Order?	
第四课	我迷路了	15
Lesson 4	I am Lost on the Road	
第五课	春夏秋冬	19
Lesson 5	Spring, Summer, Autumn and Winter	
第六课	你妈妈要你买什么？	23
Lesson 6	What Did Your Mom Ask You to Buy?	
第七课	动物园	27
Lesson 7	The Zoo	
第八课	我生病了	31
Lesson 8	I am Sick	
第九课	拆礼物	35
Lesson 9	Unwrapping Gifts	
第十课	新年快乐	39
Lesson 10	Happy New Year	
	听力练习文本	43
	Scripts for Listening Exercises	

第一课
Lesson 1

你暑假过得怎么样?
How Did Your Summer Vacation Go?

I. 听力练习 Listening Exercise

陈国和李丽正在做他们的中文暑假作业。听他们的对话并和一位伙伴讨论下列问题。

Chen guo and Li Li are doing their summer Chinese homework together. Listen to their conversation and discuss the questions listed below with a partner.

问题 Questions:

1. 陈国不懂哪些汉字？这些字的英文翻译是什么？
   What Chinese words doesn't Chen Guo understand? What are the meanings of the words in English?
2. 为什么李丽不能教陈国写汉字？
   Why can't Li Li teach Chen Guo how to write the Chinese characters?
3. 李丽和陈国计划下次什么时候见？见面的目的是什么？
   When do Li Li and Chen Guo plan to meet next time? What is the purpose of meeting?
4. 陈国说了什么来感谢李丽？
   What did Chen Guo say to express his gratefulness to Li Li at the end of the conversation?

II. 会话练习 Speaking Exercise

今天是暑假结束后第一天上课。你很高兴见到你的朋友们。加入小组并问你的朋友们他们暑假过得怎么样。

Today is the first day of class after your summer vacation. You are excited to see your friends in class. Work in small groups and ask your friends how their summer went.

他们写完了暑假作业了吗?

Did they finish their summer Chinese homework?

他们有不懂的汉字吗?

Are there Chinese words in the homework they don't understand?

他们暑假工作吗?

Did they work during the summer?

他们去看了家人吗?

Did they visit any relatives or friends?

他们去了夏令营了吗?

Did they go to any summer camps?

他们在夏令营学了什么?

What skills did they learn in the camps?

练习结束后你的老师会请你说说你的朋友们暑假做了什么。

When you finish, your teacher will ask you to tell the class what your friends did during the summer.

III. 阅读练习 Reading Exercise

你的笔友林文写给你一封信,告诉你他暑假做了什么。读林文的信并和一位伙伴回答下列问题。

Your pen pal Lin Wen, wrote about what he did in the summer. Read Lin Wen's letter and answer the questions below with a partner.

第一课 你暑假过得怎么样？
Lesson 1 How Did Your Summer Vacation Go?

_____ ，你好：

　　你暑假过得怎么样？这个暑假我去了墨西哥看我哥哥。我还参加了夏令营。

　　我的英文老师给我很多英文作业。我有很多英文字不懂。我可以请教你吗？请问 "of course" 是什么意思？"旧金山" 英文怎么写？

　　谢谢你的帮助！

林文

问题 Questions:

1. 林文暑假做了什么？
   What did Lin Wen do during the summer?
2. 林文的暑假作业有哪些？林文的暑假作业很多吗？
   What kind of summer homework did Lin Wen have? Was it a lot of homework for Lin Wen?
3. 林文问了哪两个英文问题？
   What are the two questions about English language Lin Wen asked?

IV. 写作练习 Writing Exercises

写信给林文，告诉他你暑假过得怎么样并回答林文的英文问题。

Use the following space to write a reply to Lin Wen. Talk about how your summer went and answer Lin Wen's English language questions.

V. 沟通练习 Communicative Exercise

分小组练习。角色扮演去了夏令营的学生。问问彼此去了哪些夏令营，在那儿学了什么。最后，问问你的组员们是不是可以教你在夏令营学的才艺。你的组员可以跟你礼貌地说好或不好。

Work in small groups. Role play students who have gone to different summer camps. Ask each other what summer camps one has gone to and what skills one has learned in the camps. At the end of the role play, ask your group members, if after class, they can teach you the skills they learned in the camps. Your group members can accept or politely turn down your request.

第二课
Lesson 2

我们保持联络!
Let's Keep in Touch!

I. 听力练习 Listening Exercise

陈龙和张爱林在公车站附近遇见。他们很长一段时间没见了。听他们的对话并和一位伙伴讨论下列问题。

Chen Long and Zhang Ailin ran into each other near a bus stop. They have not seen each other for a long time. Listen to their conversation and discuss the questions below with a partner.

问题 Questions:

1. 今天是星期几?

    What day is today?

2. 张爱林遇见陈龙时正要做什么?

    What did Zhang Ailin need to do when she ran into Chen Long?

3. 陈龙要了张爱林的什么联络资讯?

    What contact information did Chen Long ask for from Zhang Ailin?

4. 张爱林把联络资讯写在哪儿?

    Where did Zhang Ailin write down the contact information?

II. 会话练习 Speaking Exercise

陈丽是一个中国的高中交换生。在美国学习一年后,她准备回中国。两人一组。一个人扮演陈丽,另一个人扮演陈丽的美国同学。跟彼此说再见并向对方要联络资讯,包括电邮地址、即时通讯地址、电话号码和收信地址。

Chen Li is a high school exchange student from China. She is getting ready to return to China after studying for a year in the United States. Work in pairs. One acts as Chen Li and the other as Chen Li's classmate in the United States. Role play saying goodbye to each other and asking for each other's contact information including e-mail address, messenger address, cell phone number, and address before leaving.

III. 阅读练习 Reading Exercise

陈丽回中国后写了一封信给她美国的同学。读陈丽的信并和一位伙伴回答下列问题。

After Chen Li returned to China, she wrote a letter to her former classmates in the United States. Read Chen Li's letter and answer the questions below with a partner.

大家好:

    好久不见!你们好吗?我们学校开学了。我每天跟我朋友练习说英文。

    你们开学了吗?你们还是常常说中文、写汉字吗?

    我离开美国以后很想念你们。希望我们能常常用即时通讯聊天。保持联络!

陈丽

Lesson 2 Let's Keep in Touch!
第二课 我们保持联络！

问题 Questions:

1. 陈丽的学校开学了吗？
   Has Chen Li's school started?
2. 陈丽每天做什么？
   What does Chen Li do every day?
3. 陈丽问了她美国同学什么问题？
   What are the questions Chen Li asked her former classmates?
4. 陈丽的愿望是什么？
   What is Chen Li's hope stated at the end of the letter?

IV. 写作练习 Writing Exercises

扮演陈丽的美国同学并回复陈丽的信。跟陈丽打招呼。告诉她你的学校是否开学了。你是否还常常练习中文。最后，告诉她你希望能常常跟她联络。

Reply to Chen Li's letter as one of Chen Li's former classmates in the United States. Greet Chen Li, tell her if your school has started and if you still often practice Chinese. At the end of the letter, express your hope to keep in contact with her.

V. 沟通练习 Communicative Exercise

有一群朋友在机场遇见。他们要飞到不同的地方做不同的事。加入小组。写一篇对话。对话中这群朋友问彼此要去哪儿、做些什么事。他们还问了彼此的联络资讯。当你的小组准备好了对话，你的老师会请你在课堂上做角色扮演。

A small group of friends run into each other in the airport. They are going to fly to different places for different reasons. Work in small groups and write a short skit in which the friends ask each other why they are going to certain places and exchange contact information to keep in touch. When you are ready, your teacher will ask you to role-play the scenario in class.

第三课
Lesson 3

你们准备好点菜了吗?
Are You Ready to Order?

I. 听力练习 Listening Exercise

陈国和李丽正在一家饭馆看菜单。一位服务员来到他们桌前帮忙点菜。听他们的对话并和一位伙伴讨论下列问题。

Chen Guo and Li Li are reading the menu in a restaurant. The waiter comes to their table to take their order. Listen to their conversation and discuss the questions below with a partner.

问题 Questions:

1. 今天的特色菜是什么?
   What is today's special?
2. 这家饭馆的招牌菜是什么?
   What is the signature dish?
3. 李丽点了什么?
   What did Li Li order?
4. 陈国点了什么?
   What did Chen Guo order?

II. 会话练习 Speaking Exercise

昨天林丽丽和她的父母在一家中国饭馆吃饭。下列图画展示出吃饭的情景。四人一组。一个人扮演服务员。一个人扮演林丽丽的妈妈。一个人扮演林丽丽的爸爸。一个人扮演林丽丽。用下列图画引导你的对话。你的小组准备好时,你的老师会请你在课堂上做角色扮演。

Lin Lili and her parents ate in a Chinese restaurant yesterday. The pictures below illustrate the scenes in the Chinese restaurant. Work in groups of four. One acts as the waiter, one as Lin Lili's mother, one as Lin Lili's father, and one as Lin Lili. Use the pictures to guide your conversation. When you are ready, your teacher will ask you to role-play the scenes in front of class.

第三课 你们准备好点菜了吗?
Lesson 3 Are You Ready to Order?

III. 阅读练习 Reading Exercise

你的笔友林文搬家搬到了中国的另一个城市。他写给你一封信告诉你他试了一家新的饭馆。读林文的信并和一位伙伴回答下列问题。

Your pen pal, Lin Wen, moved to a new city in China and wrote to you recently to talk about a new restaurant he tried. Read Lin Wen's letter and answer the questions below with a partner.

大家好：

    昨天我去一家美国饭馆吃饭。这家饭馆的服务员很好。他问我喜不喜欢我的座位。这家饭馆的特色菜是羊肉汉堡，招牌菜是烤猪排。我点了羊肉汉堡和可口可乐。这家饭馆的特色菜真好吃！

    明年你来中国看我，我们一定要去这家美国饭馆吃饭！

林文

问题 Questions:

1. 林文昨天去了哪家饭馆？
   To which restaurant did Lin Wen go yesterday?
2. 服务员对林文好吗？
   Was the waiter nice to Lin Wen?
3. 服务员问了林文什么问题？
   What question did the waiter ask Lin Wen?
4. 这家饭馆的特色菜和招牌菜是什么？
   What are the restaurant's special and signature dishes?
5. 这家饭馆的特色菜好吃吗？
   Was the restaurant's special delicious?
6. 在信的最后林文建议了什么？
   What did Lin Wen suggest at the end of his letter?

Lesson 3 Are You Ready to Order?

IV. 写作练习 Writing Exercises

你是一位在饭馆打工的服务员。你每天的工作之一是写这家饭馆的招牌菜、每日的特色菜和饮料。把下列空格当作黑板。写下上述的资讯。写完后给你的同学们看并大声读出你写的资讯。

You are working as a part-time waiter or waitress in a restaurant. One of your daily tasks is to write the restaurant's signature dish, the day's special, and drinks offered on the restaurant's chalkboard. Use the space below as the chalkboard. Write down the information listed above. When you finish, show the chalkboard space to your class and read aloud the information written on it.

V. 沟通练习 Communicative Exercise

三或四人一组一起完成下面的任务。

Work in groups of 3 or 4 and complete the following task.

（1）设计饭馆菜单：菜单包括饭馆的招牌菜、每日的特色菜和其他菜色和饮料。

Design a restaurant menu: The menu should include the restaurant's signature dish, today's special, and any other dishes and drinks you may offer.

（2）扮演服务员和客人在餐厅点菜的情景。

One of you acts as a waiter or waitress and the rest of you are customers. Act out typical scenes in restaurants using the menu you designed.

（3）准备好时，你的老师会请你的小组在课堂上做角色扮演。

When you are ready, your teacher will call your group to act out the restaurant scenes in front of the class.

第四课
Lesson 4

我迷路了
I am Lost on the Road

I. 听力练习 Listening Exercise

李丽第一次要到美国大学,但是中途迷路了。她跟一些行人问路。听李丽和行人的对话并和一位伙伴讨论下列问题。

Li Li is going to visit America University for the first time and is lost on the way there. She tries to ask different passers-by for directions. Listen to Li Li's conversation with the passers-by and discuss the questions below with a partner.

问题 Questions:

1. 跟李丽交谈的第一个行人知道美国大学怎么走吗?他说了什么?
   Does the first passer-by Li Li talked with know the directions to the university? What was his response?

2. 跟李丽交谈的第二个行人知道美国大学怎么走吗?他说了什么?
   Does the second passer-by Li Li talked with know the directions to the university? What was his response?

3. 跟李丽交谈的第三个行人是谁?
   Who was the third person Li Li talked with for direction?

4. 美国大学怎么走？
What are the directions to get to America University?

II. 会话练习 Speaking Exercise

　　下方列出的是李小明现在居住的城市地图。李小明现在在他的学校外面。有一个游客来跟他问路。游客不知道中央公园、动物园、博物馆和美术馆怎么走。两人一组。一个人扮演李小明，另一个人扮演游客。游客要向李小明问路。李小明要用下面的地图跟游客说明这些地方怎么走。

　　Listed below is a map of the city Li Xiaoming currently lives in. While Li Xiaoming is standing outside his school, a tourist comes up to him to ask for directions of several places: 中央公园, 动物园, 博物馆, and 美术馆 which the tourist wants to visit. Work in pairs. One acts as Li Xiaoming and the other as the tourist. The tourist needs to ask for directions of the places mentioned above and Li Xiaoming needs to use the map below to give directions.

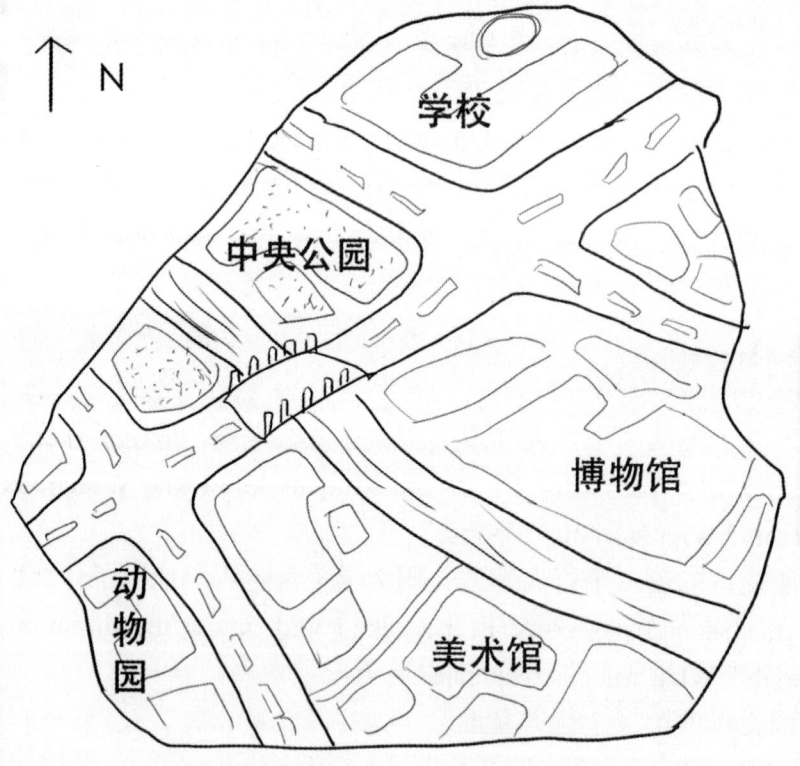

第四课 我迷路了
Lesson 4　I am Lost on the Road

III. 阅读练习 Reading Exercise

今天你的笔友林文想去一个生日派对,但是他迷路了。读林文描述他怎么迷路的信并和一位伙伴回答下列问题。

Today your pen pal, Lin Wen, wanted to go to a birthday party, but was lost on the way to the party. Read Lin Wen's letter about being lost on the road and answer the questions below with a partner.

你好:

　　今天晚上我想参加我的好朋友王红的生日会,但是我迷路了。王红的家在大学路,但是我找不到。我问路人大学路怎么走,但是路人也不知道。最后我打电话问王红,也找到她家了,但是我也迟到了!

　　　　　　　　　　　　　　　　　　　　林文

问题 Questions:

1. 林文想去谁的生日派对?

   Who birthday party did Lin Wen try to attend?

2. 林文在去生日派对的路上迷路了吗?

   Did Lin Wen get lost on the way to the birthday party?

3. 林文怎么问路?

   How did Lin Wen find the directions to the party?

4. 林文准时到了派对还是迟到了?

   Was Lin Wen on time or late to the party?

IV. 写作练习 Writing Exercises

回信给林文。告诉她你迷路的经验。

In the reply to Lin Wen, describe your experience of getting lost on the road while on the way to visit someone or some place.

 **V. 沟通练习 Communicative Exercise**

分小组练习。你的小组至少要有一个游客、一个保安、一个行人和一个加油站服务员。写一问路的短篇对话并在课堂上做角色扮演。

Work in small groups. Your groups should include at least a tourist, a policeman, a passer-by, and a gas station staff. Write a short skit about asking for directions on the road and role-play the skit in class.

第五课
Lesson 5

春夏秋冬
Spring, Summer, Autumn and Winter

I. 听力练习 Listening Exercise

李丽和陈国在冰淇淋店买冰淇淋。听他们和店员的对话并和一位伙伴讨论下列问题。

Li Li and Chen Guo are buying ice cream in an ice cream store. Listen to their conversation with the store staff and discuss the questions below with a partner.

问题 Questions:

1. 冰淇淋店有哪两种巧克力口味的冰？
   What are the two kinds of chocolate flavored ice cream the store has?
2. 李丽点了什么口味？
   What flavor did Li Li order?
3. 陈国点了什么口味？
   What flavor did Chen Guo order?
4. 李丽和陈国共付了多少钱？
   How much is the total amount Li Li and Chen Guo paid for their ice cream?

II. 会话练习 Speaking Exercise

找一个喜欢春天、一个喜欢夏天、一个喜欢秋天和一个喜欢冬天的同学。一个一个访问他们并问他们为什么喜欢某个季节。你可以把他们的答案写在下方。当你准备好时,你的老师会请你在课堂上报告结果。

Find four classmates: One likes spring, one likes summer, one likes autumn, and one likes winter. Interview them one by one and ask why they like the season. You can write down notes about what they say below. When you finish the interviews, your teacher will ask you to report your findings in class.

_____最喜欢春天,因为_____。

_____最喜欢夏天,因为_____。

_____最喜欢秋天,因为_____。

_____最喜欢冬天,因为_____。

III. 阅读练习 Reading Exercise

你的笔友林文在信里提到他最喜欢的季节。读林文的信并和一位伙伴回答下列问题。

Your pen pal, Lin Wen, talked about his favorite season in his letter. Read Lin Wen's letter and answer the questions below with a partner.

你好:

我很高兴冬天到了,因为冬天是我最喜欢的季节。我可以常常去山上滑雪,也可以做雪人。在冬天我也可以庆祝中国新年。

春、夏、秋、冬,你最喜欢哪一个季节?你也喜欢冬天吗?

林文

Lesson 5 Spring, Summer, Autumn and Winter
第五课　春夏秋冬

问题 Questions:

1. 哪个季节到了？
   Which season has arrived?
2. 林文最喜欢的季节是什么？
   What is Lin Wen's favorite season?
3. 林文在他最喜欢的季节做哪些活动？
   What activities does Lin Wen like to do in his favorite season?
4. 林文在信里问了哪两个问题？
   What are the two questions Lin Wen asked in the letter?

IV. 写作练习 Writing Exercises

回林文的信。信中写出你最喜欢的季节、在你最喜欢的季节你会做哪些活动并写出为什么你喜欢某个季节。

Write about your favorite season, what activities you would do in your favorite season, and why you like the season in the reply to Lin Wen.

V. 沟通练习 Communicative Exercise

中秋节到了。很多人在店里买月饼。分小组练习。写一短篇店员和客人的对话。店员要跟客人说店里有什么口味的月饼和月饼的价钱。客人要跟店员说想买什么月饼并问价钱。当你准备好时,你的老师会请你在课堂上做角色扮演。

It is Mid-Autumn Festival and a lot of people are shopping for moon cakes in the bakery. Work in small groups to write a skit and role-play bakers and customers. The bakers need to offer information about the moon cake flavors and prices and the customers need to decide what flavors they want to buy and ask for the prices. When you are ready, your teacher will ask you to role-play in class.

第六课
Lesson 6

你妈妈要你买什么？
What Did Your Mom Ask You to Buy?

I. 听力练习 Listening Exercise

陈国在买东西，但是他找不到一些他需要的东西。他正在问店员这些东西在哪儿。听他们的对话并和一位伙伴讨论下列问题。

Chen Guo is grocery shopping, but couldn't find several of the items he needs. He is asking a staff member in the grocery store about the items. Listen to their conversation and discuss the questions below with a partner.

问题 Questions:

1. 店里的鸡肉在哪儿？

    Where is the chicken located in the store?

2. 店里的苹果在哪儿？

    Where are apples located in the store?

3. 店里还有西瓜和苹果吗？

    Are there still watermelons and apples in the store?

4. 哪个东西明天下午三点会进货？

    What item will be restocked after 3 pm tomorrow?

我们说中文·中级1

 **II. 会话练习 Speaking Exercise**

两人一组。一个人扮演爸爸或妈妈,另一个人扮演小孩。爸爸或妈妈要告诉小孩他要小孩到店里买什么。小孩要把这些东西写下来并在课堂上报告。

Work in pairs. One acts as a parent and the other as a child. The parent needs to tell the child what items he or she wants the child to buy in the store. The child needs to write down notes about the items and report to the class what the parent wants him or her to buy.

 **III. 阅读练习 Reading Exercise**

你的笔友林文在信中提到他最近买东西的经验。读林文的信并和一位伙伴回答下列问题。

Your pen pal, Lin Wen, talked about his recent grocery shopping trip. Read Lin Wen's letter and answer the questions below with a partner.

你好:

　　昨天我和我家人一起庆祝中秋节。昨天早上我先去月饼店买了中秋月饼,下午又去超市买了牛肉和饮料。昨天晚上,我和我家人一起烤肉、吃中秋月饼、喝饮料。
　　中秋节快乐!

　　　　　　　　　　　　　　　　　　　　　　　林文

问题 Questions:

1. 林文庆祝了什么节日?
   What holiday did Lin Wen celebrate?
2. 昨天早上林文买了什么?
   What did Lin Wen buy yesterday morning?

24

Lesson 6 What Did Your Mom Ask You to Buy?

3. 昨天下午林文买了什么?

   What did Lin Wen buy yesterday afternoon?

4. 昨天晚上林文跟他家人做了什么?

   What did Lin Wen do with his family yesterday evening?

IV. 写作练习 Writing Exercises

回林文的信。写你最近买东西的经验。你跟你父母一起去吗？你买了什么？你买东西是为了庆祝特别节日吗？你找到你想买的东西了吗？

Write your recent grocery shopping experience in the reply to Lin Wen. Did you go with your parents? What did you buy? Are the items you bought for a special event? Were you able to find all the items you wanted to buy?

V. 沟通练习 Communicative Exercise

分小组练习。两个人扮演帮父母买东西的朋友。一个人扮演店员。写一短篇买东西的对话。当你准备好了,你的老师会请你在课堂上做角色扮演。

Work in small groups. Two of the group members act as friends whose parents ask them to grocery shop, and the third group member acts as the store staff. Write a short skit about grocery shopping using the grammar structures and vocabulary taught in this lesson. When you are ready, your teacher will ask you to role-play the skit in class.

第七课 Lesson 7

动物园 The Zoo

I. 听力练习 Listening Exercise

陈国和李丽在动物园。听他们的对话并和一位伙伴讨论下列问题。

Chen Guo and Li Li are visiting the zoo. Listen to their conversation and discuss the questions below with a partner.

问题 Questions:

1. 这家动物园有哪些区和馆？

   What areas and exhibition halls does the zoo have?

2. 李丽想看什么动物？

   What animals did Li Li want to see?

3. 陈国想看什么动物？

   What animals did Chen Guo want to see?

4. 李丽和陈国决定先看什么？再看什么？

   What animals did Li Li and Chen Guo decide to see first and last?

II. 会话练习 Speaking Exercise

你在附近的一家动物园工作。你的工作是画动物园的地图并跟游客解释地图上的地点。用下方的空格画一个地图。这家动物园有哪些区和馆？准备好如何解释地图。你的老师会请你在课堂上解释。

You work for a local zoo. Your current job assignment is to draw a map of the zoo and explain the locations on the map when people come to visit the zoo. Use the space below to draw the map. What areas, exhibition halls, and animals does the zoo have? Be ready to explain your map to your class when your teacher calls you.

III. 阅读练习 Reading Exercise

你的笔友林文在信里提到他今天去了动物园。读林文的信并和一位伙伴回答下列问题。

Your pen pal, Lin Wen, described his visit to a zoo today. Read Lin Wen's letter and answer the questions below with a partner.

第七课 动物园
Lesson 7 The Zoo

你好：

　　今天我跟我的朋友大元去了动物园。我们到游客服务中心问服务员这个动物园有哪些区。服务员说这个动物园只有两个区：美洲动物区和非洲动物区。我们先到美洲动物区看了棕熊，再到非洲动物区看了长颈鹿和狮子。最后我们在动物园里的饮料店喝果汁。这家店的果汁好好喝呀！

　　　　　　　　　　　　　　　　林文

问题 Questions:

1. 林文跟谁去动物园？
   Who did Lin Wen go to the zoo with?
2. 动物园游客中心的服务员告诉了林文什么资讯？
   What information did the staff in the information center in the zoo provide to Lin Wen?
3. 林文在动物园里看到了什么动物？
   What animals did Lin Wen see in the zoo?
4. 林文在动物园喝了什么？好喝吗？
   What did Lin Wen drink in the zoo? Was it tasty?

IV. 写作练习 Writing Exercises

　　回林文的信。写你最近到动物园的经验。你跟谁去了动物园？你买了什么票？你怎么找到动物园的资讯？你去了动物园的游客中心吗？你看到了什么动物？他们正一起玩吗？他们可爱吗？你在动物园买了食物和饮料吗？食物好吃吗？饮料好喝吗？

　　Write your recent zoo visiting experience in the reply to Lin Wen. Who did you go with to the zoo? What kind of ticket did you purchase? How did you find out the information about the zoo? Did you go to the information center in the zoo? What animals did you see? Were they playing with each other when you saw them? Were they cute? Did you buy any food or drinks in the zoo? Were they tasty?

V. 沟通练习 Communicative Exercise

分小组练习。两个人扮演动物园的游客。一个人扮演售票员。一个人扮演游客中心服务员。写一去动物园的短篇对话。

Work in small groups. Two act as visitors to the zoo, one as the ticket seller in the zoo, and one as the staff member in the information center in the zoo. Write a short skit about visiting the zoo using the grammar structures and vocabulary taught in the lesson.

第八课
Lesson 8

我生病了
I am Sick

I. 听力练习 Listening Exercise

李丽今天生病了。现在她正在看医生。听她和医生的对话并和一位伙伴讨论下列问题。

Li Li is feeling sick today and is visiting a doctor. Listen to her conversation with the doctor and discuss the questions below with a partner.

问题 Questions:

1. 李丽哪里不舒服？

   What were Li Li's symptoms?

2. 医生的诊断是什么？

   What was the doctor's diagnosis?

3. 李丽猜她为什么生病？

   What did Li Li guess that the cause of her illness was?

4. 医生说李丽应该做什么？

   What did the doctor say that Li Li should do?

5. 李丽什么时候可以出院？

   When can Li Li check out from the hospital?

II. 会话练习 Speaking Exercise

一班分成两组。一组是医生。另一组是病人。医生要找至少五个病人并问他们"你哪里不舒服"。病人得说他们哪里不舒服并问医生怎么办。医生要说病人为什么生病还要跟病人说怎么治病。

Divide the class into two groups. One group is doctors and the other is patients. The doctors need to find at least 5 patients to ask "你哪里不舒服？", and the patients need to describe their symptoms and ask the doctors what to do. The doctors need to guess the cause of the illness and explain ways to cure it.

III. 阅读练习 Reading Exercise

林文的一个家人最近生病了。在信里林文提到他很担心。读林文的信并和一位伙伴回答下列问题。

One of Lin Wen's family member was sick recently. Lin Wen was worried and wrote about it in his letter. Read Lin Wen's letter and answer the questions below with a partner.

你好：

　　今天我妹妹生病了。她咳嗽、发烧、全身无力。医生说她得了流行性感冒。医生说我妹妹得每天早上和晚上吃一包药，也要多喝水多休息。

　　不管如何，我希望我妹妹早日康复。

　　　　　　　　　　　　　　　　　　林文

问题 Questions:

1. 林文的哪个家人生病了？
   Who was sick in Lin Wen's family?

2. 病人哪里不舒服？

What were the patient's symptoms?

3. 病人什么时候需要吃药？

When did the patient need to take medicine?

4. 除了吃药，医生说病人还得做什么？

What else did the doctor say the patient should do other than taking the medicine?

IV. 写作练习 Writing Exercises

你最近得了流行性感冒。回林文的信。在信中写你最近生病的经验。描述你哪里不舒服，还有医生说了什么。信的最后祝林文的妹妹早日康复。

You recently got the flu. Write your recent experience in the reply to Lin Wen. Describe what symptoms you had and what the doctor said to you. At the end of the letter, wish Lin Wen's sister to get well soon.

V. 沟通练习 Communicative Exercise

分小组练习。一个人扮演医生。一个人扮演病人。其他人扮演家人。写一看医生的短篇对话。对话需要提到病人哪里不舒服、医生说什么和病人多久康复。当你准备好了,你的老师会请你在课堂上做角色扮演。注意其他组的扮演。在下表写下每组病人哪里不舒服和医生说了什么?

Work in small groups. One acts as the doctor, one as the patient, and the rest as family members. Write a short skit about a doctor's visit. In the skit, you need to include the information about the patient's symptoms, the doctor's remedies and how long it takes for the patient to get well. When you are ready, your teacher will ask each of the small groups to role-play in front of class. Pay attention to other groups' plays and write down the symptoms and remedies you hear in each play in the table below.

Group #	Patient's symptoms	Doctor's remedies	Length patient will get well

第九课
Lesson 9

拆礼物
Unwrapping Gifts

I. 听力练习 Listening Exercise

今天是陈国的生日。听他和他父母的对话并和一位伙伴讨论下列问题。
Today is Chen Guo's birthday. Listen to his conversation with his parents and discuss the questions below with a partner.

问题 Questions:

1. 陈国的妈妈给陈国的礼物是什么形状的？
   What shape is the gift from Chen Guo's mother to Chen Guo?
2. 陈国的妈妈给陈国什么礼物？
   What gift did Chen Guo's mother give Chen Guo?
3. 为什么陈国的妈妈给陈国这样的礼物？
   Why did Chen Guo's mother give Chen Guo the gift?
4. 陈国的爸爸用什么包装纸包陈国的礼物？
   What color of wrapping paper did Chen Guo's father use to wrap Chen Guo's gift?
5. 陈国喜欢爸爸给他的礼物吗？
   Did Chen Guo like the gift his father gave him?

II. 会话练习 Speaking Exercise

分小组练习。一个人扮演老师。其他人扮演学生。每个学生在纸上写下一个礼物的名称,然后交给老师。老师在每张纸上写一个号码并叫每个学生抽一张纸。大家都抽完后,老师问,"谁抽到_____号礼物?请拆礼物。"抽到老师叫的号码的学生得把纸打开。其他学生得问"是什么礼物?"学生得回答纸上写的是什么礼物。

Work in small groups. One acts as the teacher and the rest as students. Each student writes down a present idea in Chinese on a piece of paper and turn in the paper to the teacher. The teacher assigns each paper a number and asks each student to draw a paper. When everyone has a paper with number in hand, the teacher needs to ask, "Who drew present ____? Please unwrap the present". The student who drew the number the teacher called needs to unfold the paper. While the student is unfolding the paper, the group needs to ask, "What is the gift?", and the student needs to tell the group the present idea written on the paper.

III. 阅读练习 Reading Exercise

你的笔友林文今天正在庆祝他的生日。读林文的信并和一位伙伴回答下列问题。

Your pen pal, Lin Wen, is celebrating his birthday today. Read Lin Wen's letter and answer the questions below with a partner.

你好:

　　今天是我的生日。我收到了爸爸妈妈和我朋友送我的生日礼物。爸爸送我一双鞋子。妈妈送我一支毛笔。我朋友送我一本英文书。这三个礼物我都很喜欢。谢谢爸爸妈妈和我的朋友!

　　　　　　　　　　　　　　　　　　　　林文

Lesson 9 Unwrapping Gifts

问题 Questions:

1. 林文收到了几个礼物？
   How many gifts did Lin Wen receive?
2. 林文的爸爸给了林文什么？
   What did Lin Wen's father give him?
3. 林文的妈妈给了林文什么？
   What did Lin Wen's mother give him?
4. 林文的朋友给了林文什么？
   What did Lin Wen's friend give him?
5. 林文喜欢他收到的礼物吗？
   Did Lin Wen like the gifts he received?

IV. 写作练习 Writing Exercises

你的生日是什么时候？你庆祝你的生日吗？上次你收到什么礼物？回林文的信。在信中描述你的生日派对和你收到的礼物。

When is your birthday? Do you celebrate your birthday? What gifts did you receive last time? Describe your birthday celebration and the gifts you received in your reply to Lin Wen.

V. 沟通练习 Communicative Exercise

圣诞节到了。分小组练习写一拆圣诞礼物的短篇对话。对话需有家人和朋友描述他们收到了什么礼物和他们给不同礼物的理由。当你准备好了,你的老师会请你在课堂上做角色扮演。

It is Christmas. Work in small groups and write a short skit about unwrapping Christmas gifts. In the skit, family members and friends need to describe what gifts they receive and the reasons they gave certain gifts to others. When you are ready, your teacher will ask you to role-play the skit in front of the class.

第十课
Lesson 10

新年快乐
Happy New Year

I. 听力练习 Listening Exercise

明天是新年庆祝会。李丽和陈国正在谈论他们庆祝会的表演。听他们的对话并和一位伙伴讨论下列问题。

Tomorrow is the New Year celebration. Li Li and Chen Guo are talking about their performances for the event. Listen to their conversation and discuss the questions below with a partner.

问题 Questions:

1. 陈国的小组打算表演什么？
   What performance is Chen Guo's group going to perform?
2. 李丽的小组会唱几首歌？
   How many songs is Li Li's group going to sing?
3. 李丽的小组会唱什么歌？
   Which song is Li Li's group going to sing?
4. 谁说他们花了很长时间练习？
   Who mentioned that they spent a lot of time practicing for the performance?

II. 会话练习 Speaking Exercise

调查你的几个同学想去哪个城市旅游和哪些地方参观。下方第一格你可以问,"你想到哪儿旅游?",第二格你可以问,"你到达以后要到哪儿旅游?",第三格你可以问"你还想去什么地方参观?"

Survey a few of your classmate on the city and tourist attractions in the city they would like to visit. For the first column, ask, "你想到哪儿旅游?", for the second column, ask, "你到达以后要到哪儿旅游?", for the third column, ask, "你还想去什么地方参观?"

City	Tourist Attraction 1	Tourist Attraction 2

III. 阅读练习 Reading Exercise

你的笔友林文描述了学校的中国新年庆祝会。读林文的信并和一位伙伴回答下列问题。

Your pen pal, Lin Wen, talked about the Chinese New Year celebration at school. Read Lin Wen's letter and answer the questions below with a partner.

第十课 新年快乐
Lesson 10　Happy New Year

你好：

　　二月十五号我和我的同学们在中国新年庆祝会上跳了中国民俗舞。我们的表演很成功，因为我们每天都花很长时间练习。我的同学们都非常喜欢我们的表演。你在中国新年庆祝会上表演了什么？

　　中国新年快乐！

林文

问题 Questions:

1. 林文什么时候在中国新年庆祝会表演？
   When did Lin Wen perform in the Chinese New Year celebration?
2. 林文和他的同学们表演了什么舞？
   What kind of dance did Lin Wen and his classmates perform?
3. 表演成功吗？
   Was the performance successful?
4. 林文的同学们喜欢他们的表演吗？
   Did Lin Wen's classmates like the performance?

IV. 写作练习 Writing Exercises

　　你在中国新年庆祝会上表演过吗？如果你没表演过,在下列空格描述你最近和同学或朋友的表演。你们为了什么活动表演？你们表演了什么？你们花了很长时间练习吗？大家都喜欢你们的表演吗？

　　Did you perform in a Chinese New Year celebration? If you didn't, describe a recent performance you did with your classmates or friends. What was the event? What performance did you give? Did you spend a lot of time practicing for the event? Did the audience like your performance?

V. 沟通练习 Communicative Exercise

分小组练习。一起决定你们的小组想到哪儿旅游来庆祝新年。写一旅游计划的短篇对话。当你准备好时,你的老师会请你在课堂上做角色扮演。

Work in small groups. Decide on a place the group is going to visit to celebrate the New Year. Write a short skit about your touring plans in the city. When you are ready, your teacher will ask you to act out the skit in class.

听力练习文本
Scripts for Listening Exercises

Lesson 1

陈国(男声)：李丽,我有一些汉字不懂。我可以请教你吗?

李丽(女声)：当然可以。

陈国(男声)："马马虎虎"是什么意思?

李丽(女声)："马马虎虎"是"So so"的意思。

陈国(男声)："收银员"呢?

李丽(女声)："收银员"是"cashier"的意思

陈国(男声)：我还有很多汉字不会写,你现在可以教我吗?

李丽(女声)：我现在得去中国餐馆工作,没有时间。明天早上好吗?

陈国(男声)：明天早上我得去音乐夏令营。明天下午怎么样?

李丽(女声)：好。明天下午见。

陈国(男声)：谢谢你的帮助!

李丽(女声)：不客气。

Lesson 2

张爱林(女声)：陈龙!好久不见!

陈　龙(男声)：好久不见,张爱林!你好吗?

张爱林(女声)：我很好。你呢?

陈　龙(男声)：我也很好。你忙吗?

张爱林(女声)：我有点儿忙。现在我得坐公交车去学校。

陈　龙(男声)：今天是星期六,为什么你还去学校?

张爱林(女声)：因为我要跟我的中国朋友们练习中文。

陈　龙(男声)：真棒!你离开以前可以给我你的电子邮件地址吗?我想给你写邮件。

张爱林(女声)：当然可以。我把我的电子邮件地址写在一张纸上吧。

Lesson 3

李　　丽(女声)：请问今天的特色菜是什么？
男服务员(男声)：今天的特色菜是牛排。
陈　　国(男声)：请问你们的招牌菜是什么？
男服务员(男声)：我们的招牌菜是炸鸡。请问你们准备好点菜了吗？
李　　丽(女声)：我们准备好点菜了。
陈　　国(男声)：我要点一份牛排。李丽，你要点什么？
李　　丽(女声)：我想点炸鸡。
男服务员(男声)：请问你们需要饮料吗？
李　　丽(女声)：我要一杯咖啡。
陈　　国(男声)：我喝水就好了。
男服务员(男声)：好，马上来。

Lesson 4

李　　丽(女声)：先生，请问美国大学怎么走？
先生一(男声)：对不起，我不知道。你问那位先生吧。
李　　丽(女声)：先生，请问美国大学怎么走？
先生二(男声)：对不起，我也不知道。你问加油站的服务员吧。
李　　丽(女声)：服务员，请问美国大学怎么走？
加油站服务员(男声)：从这里左转。过四个红绿灯以后再右转就到了。

Lesson 5

店员(女声)：你们好。请问你们想吃什么口味的冰淇淋？
陈国(男声)：李丽，你想吃什么口味的冰淇淋？
李丽(女声)：我最爱吃巧克力冰淇淋。
店员(女声)：我们的巧克力冰淇淋有两种：白巧克力和黑巧克力。你想要哪一种？
李丽(女声)：我最喜欢吃白巧克力冰淇淋。陈国，你呢？
陈国(男声)：我想吃咖啡口味的冰淇淋。请问多少钱？
店员(女声)：总共一百五十元。

Lesson 6

陈国(男声)：我找不到鸡肉,请问还有鸡肉吗?
店员(女声)：还有,鸡肉在生鲜区。
陈国(男声)：我也找不到西瓜和苹果。请问还有西瓜和苹果吗?
店员(女声)：对不起,西瓜昨天全都卖完了。我们还有苹果。苹果在水果区。
陈国(男声)：西瓜什么时候会进货?
店员(女声)：可能明天下午三点以后。

Lesson 7

陈国(男声)：李丽,你知不知道这家动物园有哪些区哪些馆?
李丽(女声)：我知道。这家动物园有美洲动物区、澳洲动物区和亚洲动物区。这家动物园也有大熊猫馆和海洋馆。
陈国(男声)：真棒! 李丽,你想去哪些区、哪些馆?
李丽(女声)：我想先去澳洲动物区看无尾熊,再去亚洲动物区看大象和猴子。你呢?
陈国(男声)：我想去大熊猫馆看大熊猫。我们先去看无尾熊、大象和猴子,再去看熊猫吧。
李丽(女声)：好! 我们走!

Lesson 8

医生(男声)：你哪里不舒服?
李丽(女声)：我腹痛、全身无力。
医生(男声)：看来你得了急性肠炎。
李丽(女声)：我猜我可能吃了过期的食物。现在怎么办?
医生(男声)：你需要在医院卧床休息,并且禁食一天。
李丽(女声)：我什么时候可以出院?
医生(男声)：明天可以出院。
李丽(女声)：谢谢医生。

Lesson 9

爸爸妈妈(男女声)：陈国! 生日快乐!

陈国(男声)：谢谢爸爸妈妈。我可以开始拆礼物吗？
妈妈(女声)：当然可以。你可以先拆我送你的礼物。我送你的礼物是方形的那个。
陈国(男声)：哇！太棒了！是一本日文杂志！
妈妈(女声)：我知道你最近很有兴趣学日文，可能需要常常读日文，所以我送你一本日文杂志。
陈国(男声)：你说得对！谢谢妈妈。
爸爸(男女声)：现在你可以拆我送你的礼物。我送你的礼物是有蓝色包装的那个。
陈国(男声)：哇！是一顶帽子！
爸爸(男声)：我知道你很喜欢黑色帽子，所以我买了一顶黑色帽子给你。
陈国(男声)：谢谢爸爸。我很喜欢这顶帽子！
爸爸妈妈(男女声)：生日快乐！

Lesson 10

李丽(女声)：陈国，你们小组准备在新年庆祝会上表演什么？
陈国(男声)：我们小组准备表演跳舞。
李丽(女声)：你们打算跳什么舞？
陈国(男声)：我们打算跳国际标准舞。
李丽(女声)：你们的表演一定会很精彩。
陈国(男声)：希望如此。我们花了很长时间练习。你们小组打算表演什么？
李丽(女声)：我们打算唱一首歌。
陈国(男声)：什么歌？
李丽(女声)：女神卡卡的扑克脸。
陈国(男声)：真有意思。